Transforming the Ivory Tower

This volume is lovingly dedicated to my beautiful nieces: Keisha, Rebecca and Jessica. I am so very proud of each of you, for the unique qualities you possess, for the determination and resilience you have already shown, and for the joy you have brought me by having you all in my life. Despite the challenges you have already overcome, I hope this book prepares you for obstacles you may yet face in the future. I hope this book inspires you to be ambitious and bold; to have the courage to take a stand when needed and to always walk proudly with your head held high. I hope the stories of transformation show you what Black women can achieve for ourselves and others. This book is my legacy to you and your daughters that faith, hope and love has made possible. Now reach for the stars!

Deborah Gabriel

Transforming the Ivory Tower

Models for gender equality and social justice

Edited by Deborah Gabriel

tb

Trentham
Books

is an imprint of

UCL

IOE Press

First published in 2020 by the UCL Institute of Education Press, University College London, 20 Bedford Way, London WC1H 0AL

www.ucl-ioe-press.com

British Library Cataloguing in Publication Data:
A catalogue record for this publication is available from the British Library

ISBNs
978-1-85856-677-1 (paperback)
978-1-85856-913-0 (PDF eBook)
978-1-85856-914-7 (ePub eBook)
978-1-85856-915-4 (Kindle eBook)

Typeset by Servis Filmsetting Ltd, Stockport, Cheshire
Printed by CPI Group (UK) Ltd, Croydon, CR0 4YY
Cover image © smartboy10/iStockphoto.com

Contents

Notes on contributors

Deborah Gabriel is a full time academic at Bournemouth University specializing in race, gender, culture, media and communication and a consultant in educational equity, diversity and inclusion. Her work is focused on social transformation in higher education and the wider society. She is the founder and director of Black British Academics, a global network of scholars committed to enhancing racial equity in higher education, leading research on race and gender inequality and innovation in education practice through the Ivory Tower project and the 3D Pedagogy Framework. Her research interests are interdisciplinary and broadly focused on the dynamics of race, gender and culture in media, communication and higher education. These areas of inquiry are approached from a critical race and Black feminist standpoint to analyse the relationships between race, power, privilege and inequity. Deborah is an award-winning academic, receiving both student and community awards in academic excellence and teaching.

Deborah N. Brewis is a lecturer in Organization Studies at the University of Bath. She works across three interrelating themes: identifying the root rationalities of practices that organize difference and their implications, digital social media labour and digital resistance, and modes of writing differently in academic work. She examines practices of anti-racism and solidarity, gendered and racialized inequalities, dynamics of affect in relation to change, and interrogates the inequalities of the workplace, higher education, and neoliberal capitalism more generally. Her work has been published in *Organization Studies, Gender Work and Organization* and *Management Learning*.

Virginia Cumberbatch is a creative, scholar and organizer whose work sits at the intersection of community advocacy, storytelling and faith-centred social justice. She is director of Equity and Community Advocacy for the Center for Community Engagement at the University of Texas at Austin, and co-founder of Rosa Rebellion, a platform for creative activism by and for women of colour. She holds a BA in History from Williams College and an MA in Public Policy from the University of Texas. She is co-author of *As We Saw It: The Story of Integration at the University of Texas at Austin,* and is the recipient of the 2016 Anti-Defamation League Social Justice Award, the 2018 Austin 40 Under 40 Award and the 2019 Girl Scouts Women of Distinction Award for her work in community advocacy.

Sadhvi Dar is a senior lecturer in Corporate Social Responsibility and Business Ethics at Queen Mary University of London. Her research critiques colonial power structures and how these organize knowledge and subjects across contemporary institutional settings. Her activism is driven by her desire to build principled spaces for marginalized communities of colour where solidaristic relations can be re-imagined and strengthened. Since 2005 she has been organizing decolonizing and anti-racist interventions at various management and organization studies conferences and with a number of higher education institutions. Her scholarship has appeared in *Human Relations*.

Angela Martinez Dy is a lecturer in Entrepreneurship at the Institute for Innovation and Entrepreneurship, Loughborough University London. She holds a BA (Hons) in Mathematics and Creative Writing, and an MA (Dist) and PhD in Entrepreneurship. She describes herself as a poet, femcee, organizer and educator with a history of building and growing community-based organizations, including Youth Speaks Seattle, a vehicle for young people's empowerment through arts education. Her research interests and scholarly communities centre around digital entrepreneurship, anti-racist and intersectional feminism, and critical realist philosophy. She sits on the board of the Centre for Critical Realism and has published in *Human Relations*, *Organization, Gender, Work and Organization*, and the *International Small Business Journal*.

William Lez Henry is Professor of Criminology and Sociology at the School of Human and Social Sciences at the University of West London. His areas of expertise are criminology, sociology, anthropology, race, education, ethnicity, youth crime and cultural studies. In addition to his academic career, Professor Henry is reggae DJ Lezlee Lyrix, a writer, poet and community activist who has been interviewed extensively for television and radio.

Ima Jackson is a community-engaged researcher working broadly within migration. Her research has developed through sustained engagement with communities of colour in Scotland, including those that are newly migrated. She works regularly across portfolios with Scottish Government ministers, their civil servants and policy-makers. Over the last twenty years, as unprecedented migration has changed Scotland's demography, her work has developed from the experiences of those who are often marginalized by systems of policy development and service provision. Ima's work is focused on social justice and draws on the authority and integrity of the academy to support communities in evidencing their experiences through research to policy- and decision-makers, with the aim of increasing their representation and participation in social research.

Josephine Kwhali has an extensive background in social work education and training, initially working in practice before moving on to middle and senior management positions where she was involved in a number of the profession's equality initiatives. Josephine subsequently worked at Lincoln, Kent, Wolverhampton and Coventry universities, specializing in child protection and race equality, and lecturing and researching on both. She undertook her doctorate at Sussex University, researching what anti-racist social work practice might learn from Black theology and the narratives of Black Christian elders. She currently works on a consultancy and freelance basis.

Helena Liu is a senior lecturer at UTS Business School in Sydney, Australia. Her research critiques the way power sustains our enduring romance with leadership and imagines the possibilities for organizing through solidarity, love and justice. She is currently a co-chief investigator on the Australian Research Council Discovery project, Leadership Diversity Through Relational Intersectionality in Australia. She serves as associate editor at *Human Relations*, *Management Learning* and *Equality, Diversity and Inclusion*. In addition to those journals, her work has also appeared in *Organization, Journal of Business Ethics, Gender, Work and Organization, Culture and Organization*, and *Leadership*. Her first book, *Redeeming Leadership: An Anti-Racist Feminist Intervention*, was published in January 2020.

Elizabeth Opara is an associate professor in the Faculty of Science, Engineering and Computing at Kingston University London. She obtained her BSc (Hons) in Medical Biochemistry from Royal Holloway, University of London, and her DPhil in Biochemistry from the University of Oxford. She is currently Head of Department of Applied and Human Sciences and co-leader of the Sport, Exercise, Nutrition and Public Health Research Group. She has been an academic for more than twenty years and, in addition to teaching and research, she is committed to using her experiences in higher education to guide and mentor other academics.

Aisha Richards is an academic and creative practitioner. She is the founder and director of Shades of Noir, an independent programme delivered across the University of the Arts London and other institutions. It aims to enhance education and arts practice in higher education by developing resources, providing spaces and offering accessible knowledge and visibility for staff, students, graduates and creative practitioners. She co-authored the HEA (Higher Education Academy) guides *Retention and Attainment in the Disciplines: Art and Design* and *Embedding Equality and Diversity in the Curriculum: An Art and Design Practitioner's Guide*. Aisha also consults on institutional change management, pedagogical practice and curriculum development.

Udeni Salmon is a research fellow at the University of Lincoln and an honorary research associate at the University of Keele. Her PhD was awarded from the University of Salford in 2017. Prior to her academic career, Udeni spent twenty years working in senior positions at Deloitte Consulting, IBM and Leonard Cheshire Disability. Udeni's research interests are concerned with how power manifests itself in organizational relationships. She uses intersectionality, critical race theory, Black feminist theory and Bourdieusian theory to inform her work. She writes in the areas of family firms, entrepreneurship, innovation, and modern slavery.

Shirley Anne Tate is Professor in the Sociology Department at the University of Alberta, Canada, where she is Canada Research Chair Tier 1 (designate) in Feminism and Intersectionality. She was formerly Professor of Race and Education, founder and director of the Centre for Race, Education and Decoloniality in the Carnegie School of Education at Leeds Beckett University, UK. She is Honorary Professor, Chair for Critical Studies in Higher Education Transformation at Nelson Mandela University, South Africa, and

Visiting Professor at the Swedish School of Social Sciences, University of Helsinki, Finland. Her area of research is broadly Black Diaspora studies, with research interests in institutional racism, the body, affect, beauty, race performativity, Caribbean decolonial studies, and the intersections of race and gender.

Acknowledgements

My late maternal grandmother, Wilhelmina Harriott (1902–2005), never attended university, yet the knowledge and wisdom she imparted to me in my adult years has shaped my academic life more profoundly than anything gleaned through my primary, secondary and tertiary educational experiences in the UK. Wilhelmina connected me with my cultural and ancestral history, which not only helped me locate my place in the world and appreciate the contributions of her generation to human history but also inspired me to build on those foundations. Wilhelmina gave me the greatest gift in life that has enabled me to survive and thrive: faith, hope and love, all essential to the human spirit. Wilhelmina bestowed upon me intellectual, social and cultural capital that inspired my creation of Black British Academics, and subsequently the Black Sister Network and the Ivory Tower project. It is therefore entirely appropriate to acknowledge her otherwise invisible contribution to this legacy.

As the youngest of five children I found the role of my siblings, Audrey, Jennifer, Rosemarie and Dave, really important to my education and socialization. They blessed me with kindness, unconditional love, encouragement and support, reminding me of my value and worth as a Black woman. Crucially, they correct me when I am wrong, they provide constructive criticism, alternative perspectives and engaged dialogue on various social issues. In so doing, they contribute to my intellectual development through conversational learning, in addition to imbuing me with a sense of belonging. It is therefore important for me to acknowledge their contribution to this volume.

Black British Academics is a growing network of scholars and activists within and beyond the higher education sector who are committed to racial justice and equity in both the academy and wider society. It is a movement for social transformation that operates as a collective, though often through individual acts of resistance in teaching, research, professional and community practice that is not always supported, valued or rewarded within higher education institutions or the industries they serve. The Black Sister Network is built on sisterhood and solidarity aimed at empowering Black women and women of colour. While both volumes in the Ivory Tower project aim to highlight the experiences, perspectives, contributions and achievements of this collective, there are many more stories and case studies than the ones they feature that also speak to these efforts to challenge Whiteness, privilege and inequality. This book is therefore both an acknowledgement and a celebration of these endeavours.

I am privileged and grateful to have collaborated with so many amazing women on both volumes. In addition to all the contributors, this gratitude is extended to the peer reviewers, production and marketing team at UCL IOE Press, especially Gillian Klein, co-founder and publisher of Trentham Books, for her dedication, support and commitment to bringing often-marginalized critical voices to the wider public.

Deborah Gabriel

Foreword
William Lez Henry

You may be wondering why a man is writing the foreword to a book that clearly seeks to challenge the dominant male gaze, as well as the centrality of whiteness in the struggles of Black women and women of colour to decolonize, in this instance, academia. I can offer a two-fold explanation here. The first speaks to how during the 1990s a Yoruba sistren[1] invited me to a gathering at her home and introduced me to her mother, who I ended up reasoning with for some time. The next day my sistren told me that her mother had said speaking to me reminded her of sitting at the feet of the wise old women back home. For me, this was the ultimate compliment as it spoke to my belief that I am merely an ancestral vessel, channelling in this place and at this time. The second speaks to the first time I met *Sis Debs* (as I have always called her, denoting our kinship). It was 2006. I was a lecturer at Goldsmiths, she was an undergraduate student and journalist and interviewed me for an article on, ironically, racism in academia. I was totally blown away by her intellectual rigour and passion for social justice for the disenfranchised and disaffected African Diaspora. While walking with her to exit the campus, I told her: 'Sis Debs, you need to do a PhD. If you really want to make a difference and use that intellect and passion, do a PhD'. She later told me that my encouragement motivated her to undertake a doctorate. I am honoured to be regarded as a mentor as well as a lifelong friend to Sis Debs, and to add this small contribution to what is a timely, necessary, profoundly insightful and novel second take on the myriad struggles of sisters within the Ivory Tower, as detailed in this wonderful book.

In this edited collection, Gabriel successfully builds on the inroads made by *Inside the Ivory Tower*, which sought to place a counter-narrative within the heart of academia as a space dominated by 'whiteness and patriarchy', while maintaining the individuality, clout and potency of the voices of the contributors. Consequently, this collection of essays, reasonings, musings and self-reflections represents far more than a mere 'academic enterprise'. It is an uncompromising and very necessary addition to the ongoing 'political mission' to hold the chief beneficiaries of White privilege to account. This is achieved by shifting the focus to an epistemologically privileged position from which the standpoints of Black women and women of colour gain centrality in the debate on how to transform the Ivory Tower, because the registers and measures utilized here are grounded within self-generated concepts (Lewis, 2006) which position the perspectives within a Black feminist framework that challenge the authority of the White middle-class male as 'knower'.

From this Black feminist standpoint, the authors advance powerful, authoritative arguments enriched by the breadth of anecdotal evidence and the divergent and novel way the book is constructed, where we are introduced to personal narratives from the front line. More importantly, the sense of sisterhood, love, care and active involvement at grassroots as well as academic level is the central thread throughout the book, where recognizing that as a Black woman or woman of colour your predicament often renders you vulnerable. For this reason, the Black Sister Network, 3D Pedagogy Framework (Gabriel), Building the Anti-Racist Classroom (Brewis *et al.*), Black Women Science Networks (Opara) and Teaching Within programme (Richards) not only offer viable ways of challenging discriminatory practices within and beyond academia, but also offer tangible ways to heal by providing a form of ontological security (Laing, 1961; Giddens, 1991) in spaces where a sense of freedom can be gained from what Kwhali describes as 'the pit of racial oppression'.

Through internationally diverse perspectives this book offers valuable insights that introduce us to alternative ways to map and track city and community life beyond the four walls of the classroom in the tradition of the very visible 'flâneurs' (Alexander, 1976). For example, Cumberbatch, in conversation with Gabriel, explains why in Austin, Texas, the 'Front Porch Gathering' was introduced as a means to give those most affected by 'cultural erasure and gentrification' a central and active voice through a research project entitled Those Who Have Stayed. Cumberbatch's notion of 'community recalibration' is an approach that all universities should embrace, especially when it is pertinent to consider what research impact should look like and what it should achieve at the interface between theory and praxis.

In a similar vein, Jackson's chapter on FGM (female genital mutilation) policy in Scotland highlights how a Black feminist standpoint informed community research that enabled women to actively engage as equals in a 'co-creative partnership'. Jackson's approach helped women to overcome feelings of marginalization and succeed in developing new knowledge through a mechanism that allowed their voices to be centred and respected. Universities that wish to serve their local communities in pragmatic and practical ways can adopt this model to challenge Eurocentric norms in which knowledge generation and dissemination are the sole purview of privileged White academics.

In her chapter, Kwhali suggests that we acknowledge the relevance of gleaning self-knowledge from forms of racial oppression, then share it with others who are making their collective contributions, otherwise there is a real danger that the oppressed will individualize their predicament and then internalize that oppressive situation. In their chapter, Brewis *et al.* demonstrate why this perspective is so important; it is not solely based on resisting racial oppression but transcending it by creating and controlling the direction of their BARC initiative. The individual, autoethnographic insights they provide on how they arrived at a place of safety and solidarity that gave life to BARC is welcomed because the utilization of women of colour is fully explained. This chronological narrative is crucial, because too often universities utilize a nebulous take on women of colour to promote, and more importantly celebrate, a vulgar type of diversity and inclusion that ultimately legislates and militates against Black women. Thus, it undermines the very notion of sisterhood that is crucial to 'decoloniality and intersectional feminism' as argued by Gabriel and Tate in conversation.

Transforming the Ivory Tower is an essential and accessible read for scholars, activists and anyone who operates at a grassroots level, who seeks to effect critical change in their area of expertise. This book does not pander to fitting into the staid and scholastic frameworks that speak exclusively to academics in language that is so convoluted as to exclude a wider audience, thereby limiting the dissemination of knowledge. Throughout this volume there is an emphasis on inclusivity, first through a notion of sisterhood that is pragmatically feminist, viable, doable and necessary to decentralize the dominant White male gaze. Second, contributors like Kwhali highlight the importance of acknowledging personhood in line with a womanist take on recognizing the commonalities of our collective condition as the main recipients of the deleterious effects of White privilege within academia. I therefore end this foreword with a quote from Kwhali's chapter, which encapsulates Gabriel's vision for this profoundly insightful book:

> Racism is no respecter of age, generation or geographical location. My testimony in this chapter, in its essence if not in detail, will surely find resonance with many of my sisters (and hopefully brothers) who are making their own individual and collective contributions.

References

Alexander, S. (1976) 'Women's work in nineteenth-century London: A study of the years 1820–1850'. In Mitchell, J. and Oakley, A. (eds) *The Rights and Wrongs of Women*. London: Penguin.

Giddens, A. (1991) *Modernity and Self-Identity: Self and society in the late modern age*. Stanford, CA: Stanford University Press.

Laing, R.D. (1961) *Self and Others*. London: Tavistock Publications.

Lewis, R., cited in Henry, W. ('Lez') (2006) *What the Deejay Said: A critique from the street!* London: Learning By Choice Publications.

Endnote

[1]In Rastafari/Jamaican we use 'sistren' for sister and 'bredrin' for bother.

Introduction
Deborah Gabriel

In common with its predecessor *Inside the Ivory Tower* (published by Trentham Books in 2017, for convenience IT1), this edited volume is the outcome of an ongoing collaborative project that began in 2014, with the key aims of building solidarity and empowerment for Black women and women of colour through collective activism. The Black Sister Network within Black British Academics, the community through which this project was developed, remains a space of proactive participation, critical reflection, innovation, love, support and sisterhood. While IT1 is primarily concerned with helping readers develop a critical consciousness around our lived experience of raced and gendered discrimination within academia, *Transforming the Ivory Tower* (IT2) is focused on our contributions to teaching, research, professional and community practice aimed at addressing race and gender disparities with a focus on tackling whiteness – a recurrent theme in IT1. This research is unique in providing case studies that highlight self-defined and negotiated pathways developed by Black women and women of colour as change-makers. It documents how we navigate spaces that are often challenging and sometimes hostile, to create meaningful roles that contribute to equity and social justice.

IT1 and IT2 share common objectives: they set out to analyse the sources and manifestations of race and gender inequality, drawing on lived experience as a powerful tool of engagement to engender the critical consciousness and promote the agency that are prerequisites for social change. However, while IT1 aims to empower women of colour by giving voice to our subjective realities, it also targets White men and women within and beyond academia in the hope that they will gain a deeper understanding of how racism manifests in our day-to-day lives within the academy and the role that whiteness and privilege play in this process. It is the critical consciousness of White men and women that we most hope to impact to transform their attitudes, behaviours and actions, to bring about positive change. Following the publication of IT1 in 2017 we collected quantitative data through a reader survey and had many responses, especially from White male academics, including professors who said they found our narratives constructive and insightful. I also had many emails from White male academics offering support and saying they had been inspired by IT1 to think differently. We hosted seven book launches at the various institutions of the contributors, attended by over 500 people in all, and did press interviews with *The Independent, The Guardian, Times Higher Education* and BBC Radio. I even took part in a BBC News report in 2018 that was broadcast on the 6 o'clock and 10 o'clock news, focusing on racial inequality in higher education.

However, as rewarding as the public engagement has been, I am mindful that this is not a measure of the social change that we strive for. In material terms, little has changed. Though we were not expecting a seismic shift, it is still frustrating that whiteness and privilege remain intact and stronger than ever. A recent study by the University and College Union (Baker, 2019) reveals that as Black academics we earn on average £7K less than our White peers. While White academics make up 84 per cent of academic staff, 93 per cent of professors are White, as are 91 per cent of managers in higher education. We remain undervalued, underpaid and unrewarded.

It perhaps raises the question as to why we continue to work in academia if the prospects are so dire. The answers can be found in this volume. More importantly, our narratives are evidence of our knowledge, skills, expertise and contributions to our institutions as well as to the wider global knowledge economy. Though we hope all readers will be inspired by our stories, this volume is primarily aimed at Black women and women of colour, including students and graduates who aspire to be academics; staff in administrative and operational roles who may aspire to be academics; and those who are already working as lecturers and researchers who struggle to find a niche where they can pursue social justice and challenge inequality. The *models for gender equality and social justice* referred to in the subtitle of this volume are examples for Black women and women of colour of how to swim against the tide, how to transform the spaces we work in and how to transform ourselves.

This research draws conceptually on critical race theory and Black feminism and adopts the emancipatory methods of autoethnography and participatory witnessing. Autoethnography privileges subjectivity and is broadly defined as 'cultural analysis through personal narrative' (Boylorn and Orbe, 2013: 17). Through the process of participatory witnessing, *witnesses* bear testimony and listen in a way that encourages self-representation. Bearing testimony is an active form of resistance against hegemony by telling one's own story and defining one's own reality. It 'involves an active engagement of the self in order to create the space in which to share in the experience of others' (Taylor, 1998: 58) in a way that validates the experience of those bearing witness. A tool within the repertoire of Black feminism, participatory witnessing promotes critical self-reflection to facilitate accurate representation of the stories being told (ibid.: 1998).

Divided into two parts, Part 1 of the book is comprised of autoethnographies, while Part 2 presents theoretical conversations centred around the transformative work of the selected contributors, followed by theoretical insights drawn from the discussions. This volume brings intersectional voices to the Ivory Tower project from the USA, Australia and Canada and from LGBTQ perspectives, while maintaining continuity in highlighting the transformative work of some of the UK contributors to IT1. This research is significant in highlighting the often-unacknowledged contributions to the higher education sector, and the narratives privilege the lived experience, intellectual, social and cultural capital of Black women and women of colour. In addition to bringing new perspectives to the Ivory Tower project, this volume also adds critical reflections from all the contributors on our experience of participating in this research. It seems fitting that as a political project aimed at promoting our growth and empowerment, an effective approach to achieving this is learning from the process of undertaking collaborative Black feminist research so that the knowledge and understandings we derive can help us to move forward.

References

Baker, S. (2019) 'Black academics "paid £7K less" than White colleagues on average'. *Times Higher Education*. Online. www.timeshighereducation.com/news/black-academics-paid-ps7k-less-white-colleagues-average (accessed 12 January 2020).

Boylorn, R.M. and Orbe, M.P. (eds) (2013) *Critical Autoethnography: Intersecting cultural identities in everyday life*. Walnut, CA: Left Coast Press.

Taylor, J.Y. (1998) 'Womanism: A methodologic framework for African American women'. *Advances in Nursing Science*, 21 (1), 53–64.

Auto-ethnographies on trans-formational scholar activism

1

Chapter 1

Teaching to transgress through 3D Pedagogy: Decolonizing, democratizing and diversifying the higher education curriculum

Deborah Gabriel

> *Progressive professors working to transform the curriculum so that it does not reflect biases or reinforce systems of domination are most often the individuals willing to take the risks that engaged pedagogy requires and to make their teaching practices a site of resistance.* (hooks, 1994:21)

Introduction

The 3D Pedagogy Framework is a strategic model of culturally democratic teaching and learning practice that I developed through Black British Academics to decolonize, democratize and diversify the higher education (HE) curriculum. It is the product of critical race and Black feminist scholarship and praxis. Its objectives are firmly encapsulated in Black feminist thought both in terms of resistance to whiteness and as a catalyst for change. Black feminist theory posits that critical thinking promotes agency and lies at the heart of engaged pedagogy as a form of political activism, while critical consciousness is a prerequisite for social change (Hill Collins, 1990; hooks; 1994). Both are central to my 3D Pedagogy Framework. This chapter reflects on my journey through its development and implementation, the challenges I have encountered both in delivering transformative teaching to predominantly White students, and in resisting its appropriation as an institutional tool to be operationalized within an increasingly marketized, bureaucratized environment where social justice is not the primary driver.

Between 2016 and 2019 I undertook consultancy work in teaching and learning for Shades of Noir, collaborating with its founder and director Aisha Richards on our Specialist Training and Delivery Programme of

Deborah Gabriel

Curriculum Development and Enhanced Teaching Practice Based on a Social Justice and Cultural Democracy Framework. The aim of our programme was to liberate the curriculum and democratize the cultural environment in which teaching and learning takes place, to enhance inclusive teaching practice and promote transformational education across University of the Arts London (UAL). This programme evolved from previous collaborations where we undertook curriculum reviews for several undergraduate and postgraduate programmes across UAL. Frustrated with the Eurocentric curriculum at my own institution in the corporate marketing communications department, I initially developed the 3D Pedagogy Framework as a means of transforming my own education practice. Later, I recognized its potential to improve the cultural competence of lecturers and enhance the experience and outcomes of students of colour, while enriching the learning process for students of all ethnic and cultural backgrounds.

My first full-time academic role in HE represented a ten-year journey from my entry as a mature undergraduate student in 2004. My experiences as an undergraduate, postgraduate student and early career researcher are documented in my chapter 'Race, racism and resistance in British academia' (Gabriel, 2016). My narrative reflected on the race and racism manifested through the whiteness of the institutional culture, environment, education policies and the curriculum, and their impact on my sense of belonging. I established Black British Academics in 2013 as a platform and network of resistance to our marginalization within the academy as people of colour, recognizing that knowledge is our most powerful tool against racial oppression. According to bell hooks (1994: 2), 'devotion to learning' is a 'counterhegemonic act'. Therefore, the fervour and intensity with which I immersed myself in critical scholarship for my doctoral thesis was both a form of political participation as well as a honing of my political skills in examining how African Caribbean people adopt digital media 'to harness social and cultural capital, to mediate against racism and marginalization within British society and to empower themselves and their communities' (Gabriel, 2016: ix). As a Black female academic I endured the same racialized experiences as the participants in my doctoral research and the strategies they adopted for their empowerment became central to the mission of Black British Academics.

Developing the 3D Pedagogy Framework as a mission for social justice

By the time I started teaching in my first full-time academic role I had already developed skills and expertise in deconstructing the curriculum and critiquing content and Eurocentric teaching styles through my consultancy activities

6

with Black British Academics for HE institutions. The undergraduate modules I inherited were devoid of any engagement with issues around race and representation, with one exception. A module I taught in my first year on media and popular culture was excellent at foregrounding race and gender and highlighting inequality and stereotyping, but it was subsequently removed from the programme. I replaced all the inherited content for modules I taught with my own learning resources, drawing on social justice pedagogy and critical race pedagogy, as documented in 'Pedagogies of social justice and cultural democracy in media higher education' (Gabriel, 2018). I had a strong desire to positively impact the learning experience of students of colour, who comprised a small minority of the undergraduates I taught. At the same time I wanted to transform the perceptions, attitudes and media practice of the majority of students in my classes, who were White. This inspired my development of the final-year undergraduate elective module, Media Inequality. My aim was first and foremost 'teaching to transgress' (hooks, 1994), which represents an ongoing mission for liberatory and transformative education. bell hooks's assertion that in contemporary education teaching reinforces rather than challenges racial stereotypes rang especially true on the programmes I taught in public relations, advertising and marketing communications. I wanted to be part of the 'pedagogy of resistance' (hooks, 1994: 2) to engage my students 'to be active participants in learning' (ibid.: 1994: 11). Most of all, I wanted my students to develop 'the critical consciousness necessary to analyse and critique problematic racialized representations in the communication industries in future employment and become agents of change' (Gabriel, 2018: 35). Media Inequality was also a direct response to the clarion call by the National Union of Students in 2012 for 'liberation' of the curriculum 'in terms of actively working to challenge and tackle structural inequalities in society' (Gabriel, 2018: 36).

On a broader level, as the founder and director of Black British Academics, I felt a responsibility to address the 'race and gendered ideologies, attitudes and behaviours' that are 'channelled through and within higher education' as argued in IT1 (Gabriel and Tate, 2017: 148) and asserted by hooks:

> If we examine critically the traditional role of the university in pursuit of truth and the sharing of knowledge and information, it is painfully clear that biases that uphold and maintain White supremacy, imperialism, sexism, and racism have distorted education so that it is no longer about the practice of freedom. (hooks, 1994: 29)

This brought me to the realization that I needed to create a model for my teaching practice that tackled three pillars of Whiteness: colonialism (decolonization), marginalization/exclusion (democratization) and domination (diversification). Early proponents of decoloniality argue that to challenge Eurocentric modes of thinking, inextricably linked to slavery, colonialism and modernity, necessitates constructing and advancing new ways of thinking, knowing and doing from the intellectual production that emerges from the lived experience of people of colour, as the colonized (Fausto Reinaga and Frantz Fanon, both cited in Walsh, 2012). My discipline – media, culture and communication – is an ideal project for decolonization. Media education can and should contribute to social justice and equity but too often perpetuates Eurocentric ideologies and epistemologies. Varied sites and uses of media, whether in a professional context such as public relations, or a personal context like social media, are paradoxically democratic spaces and ones that undermine equality by marginalizing some voices while privileging others. Take public relations (PR) for example, which grew from slavery and colonization in the nineteenth and twentieth centuries. The social, economic and political domination of African, Asian and South American nations by White European nations was reinforced by ideologies perpetuated through PR strategies that disseminated the message of White superiority. Therefore, since its inception, PR has been deeply entrenched in a global system of racial inequality (Munshi and Edwards, 2011). However, this is largely excluded from curricula. This example alone highlights the need:

> To help students critically engage with historical and contemporary issues around race, ethnicity and culture and their relationship with power across the media and in communications practice with the specific aim of facilitating their development of cultural competencies that can be applied in a professional context to a range of communication industries. (Gabriel, 2018: 39)

The inclusion of democratization in my 3D Pedagogy Framework was inspired through engaging with the work of formidable Black women scholars. As hooks (1994: 40) argues, democratizing the curriculum means paying attention to the issue of voice: 'Who speaks? Who listens? And why?' Aldridge (2000: 101) asserts that in HE, cultural democracy means including and valuing 'the complexity and variety of views which have shaped the boundaries of knowledge [and] expands rather than restricts our view of the world'. I would argue that democratizing the learning environment necessitates radical and critical interventions informed by the lived experience and knowledge of people of colour. I therefore integrate lived experience into my lectures and seminars that highlight the role of stereotypical representations in sustaining and perpetuating racial inequality at socio-cultural, political and economic levels, reflecting material inequalities. Often, I draw on examples from my own personal experience, which facilitates students' deeper engagement with the subject and actualization of critical race theory and Black feminism as the core theories of the course. Dialogical pedagogy, as outlined by Jackson (2008), is an integral component of 3D Pedagogy, therefore ensuring students share their experiences, insights and understandings of critical readings, and media outputs enable me to embed critical discussion into the course content. As hooks (1994: 39) argues, 'Making the classroom a democratic setting where everyone feels a responsibility to contribute is a central goal of transformative pedagogy'.

Diversification in the 3D Pedagogy Framework is an essential component and necessary response to epistemological racism. It has long been argued that the ideological and philosophical assumptions that underpin academia and shape mainstream curricula are largely drawn from the socio-historic experiences of White middle- and upper-class males (Aldridge, 2000; Blay, 2008; Darder, 1994; Mighty, 2001) 'through theories that are universalized and presented as THE objective, unbiased truth' (Mighty, 2001: 4). The teaching and learning environment therefore marginalizes students of colour, women and the working classes while privileging predominantly White middle- and upper-class males. Epistemological racism refers to the ways in which White European epistemologies are deeply embedded within every sphere of society to the extent that White, Western thought is always centralized and determines how knowledge is created, defined and validated (Scheurich and Young, 1997). Democratization therefore refers to the inclusion within the curriculum not only of global and diverse cultural perspectives but also of diverse teaching styles. Reading lists for most degree programmes largely comprise White male and female scholars, although the former dominate. For Media Inequality and the other modules I teach, I make a conscious effort to include scholars of colour and display photos of the academics I cite in my lectures and learning resources, to enhance their visibility.

Delivering transformative teaching through 3D Pedagogy

I taught Media Inequality for three consecutive academic years and have borne witness to its transformative potential. The first year it ran in 2016/17 was the most enjoyable and rewarding experience I have had as a lecturer. The cohort of final-year undergraduates were the most ethnically diverse and engaged of all my classes and comprised 21 students, of which exactly one-third were students of colour. At the end of the first lecture the only Black male in the class approached me. He said it was the first time he had ever been taught by a Black lecturer and asked if we could meet for a chat. I arranged to meet him for coffee two days later and when I arrived at our meeting place, with him were two Black females who were his fellow PR students. Since there was one other Black female student on their degree programme in a different seminar group to the others, I invited her along to the next coffee 'meeting'. It became a regular session. We would talk generally about their studies but also about their experiences of being Black in a predominantly White university and I would try to encourage them. We would also converse about Black issues in general and this cultural camaraderie helped increase my sense of belonging, as well as theirs. I felt maternal responsibility for these four students as their only Black female mentor at the institution, in a relationship that Hill Collins defines as 'community othermothers': Black women who make important contributions to their communities through 'connectedness with others', organizing and nurturing Black communities in ways that build common interests and inspire community activism (Hill Collins, 1990). These four students were my 'community', and each week we met to discuss social issues, an integral component of social justice pedagogy, aimed at helping students develop:

> ... critical analytical tools necessary to understand oppression and their own socialization within oppressive systems, and to develop a sense of agency and capacity to interrupt and change oppressive patterns and behaviours in themselves and in the institutions and communities of which they are a part. (Bell, 2007: 2)

At the same time I was conscious of the fact that for students of colour attending predominantly White institutions, a sense of belonging is not solely dependent on interactions within the academic environment but also on external interactions with key support networks (Hurtado and Carter, 1997). In this instance, through our weekly sessions, I became part of their external support network and thereby helped to increase their sense of belonging.

The White students in this cohort were a joy to teach. They had a genuine interest not just in the subject matter but were passionate about creating a fair and just world and we had lively and respectful discussions in the seminars. Every student in the cohort attended tutorials and would share their enthusiasm for the course. Some of the White students talked of how it enabled them to discuss issues of race with their peers and with their parents. This is a feature of 3D Pedagogy, since critical paradigms can aid students in identifying hidden inequalities and encourage them 'to be deconstructive, to question, and to problematize issues' (Mwthehwa-Sommers, 2014: 21).

I taught purposefully in a culturally democratic learning space without hierarchies of race, gender, class or sexuality, eagerly anticipating every lecture and seminar. I always left the classes smiling and feeling elated, and the joy I experienced was shared by the students who told me regularly how much they enjoyed the classes as well as what they would like more of. For example, a dual-heritage student who wanted to explore media representation of multi-racial identity said she would welcome greater inclusion of such examples in the lectures and seminars, and I made a point of adding these to the course content. 'When students see themselves as mutually responsible for the development of a learning community, they offer constructive input' (hooks, 1994: 206). The mutual joy of learning within my Media Inequality community reminded me of hooks's concept of ecstasy:

> I remember vividly the faces, gestures, habits of being of all the individual teachers who nurtured and guided me, who offered me an opportunity to experience joy in learning, who made the classroom a space of critical thinking, who made the exchange of information and ideas a kind of ecstasy. (hooks, 1994: 202)

A key objective of 3D Pedagogy is helping students develop agency and resistance, based on my conviction that students can become agents of change and that '... people in both advantaged and targeted groups have a critical role to play in dismantling oppression and generating visions for a more socially just future' (Bell, 2007: 13). To that end I have always organized extra-curricular activities on my modules that relate to current social issues:

> In week three of the 13-week [Media Inequality] unit, a BBC Radio Solent reporter attended one of the teaching sessions to record interviews for the Breakfast Show on how the unit can help bring positive changes to the advertising industry. Two students volunteered to take part in the interviews, while the remaining students contributed to the show by helping to select the adverts to be featured and providing feedback on the script that I created. They also became the audience during the recording of the show, helping to create the atmosphere of a live studio discussion. (Gabriel, 2018: 40–1)

In July 2017 I hosted a panel discussion event focused on a topic featured in Media Inequality, around race, gender and representation in the media and popular culture. The panellists included writer and broadcaster Afua Hirsch, Big Voice Communications CEO Catherine Grinyer, Shades of Noir director Aisha Richards and then Bournemouth University Marketing

Communications student Stacey Kelly-Maher. Two other students volunteered to contribute to organizing and delivering the event: Ray Taiwo and Naomi Oti-Sampson. Since the event was funded, all students were financially remunerated for their services.

The representation of Muslim communities in the media is another of the Media Inequality topics. Therefore, in the 2017/18 academic year I organized a social evening at Bournemouth Islamic Centre and Central Mosque, where students engaged directly with local people so that their understandings of the key issues would be informed through not just theory but lived experience. This was not the first time I integrated local community organizations into my teaching practice. As the leader of a module called Social Communication, I worked with Dorset Race Equality Council and together we developed an assessment where students were required to design social communication for the organization based on priority issues. In 2018 I received the Award in Academic Excellence at the first Dorset Ethnic Minority Awards.

The positive feedback I received directly from students has been replicated in formal evaluations that include statements from student course representatives at programme team meetings and in data I have collected at the end of each course for the past three years. I designed the survey to evaluate student perceptions of their cultural competencies and their potential to contribute to positive changes in the communication industries. The findings:

> demonstrate that all students had self-perceptions of high level understandings of dominant ideologies, theories on race, ethnicity and culture and White privilege, and felt more culturally competent than they did before completing the course. (Gabriel, 2018: 42)

However, the most meaningful affirmation from the students have been the awards they have conferred on me, especially in the absence of any institutional recognition. In the 2016/17 and 2017/18 academic years I received 'You're Brilliant' awards, run by our students' union where students vote for staff they feel have made an outstanding contribution to their learning and/or university experience. In 2016/17 the certificate read: 'For developing the Media Inequality unit to develop the cultural competencies of students and continuously working towards meaningful social change'. In 2017/18 the certificate read:

> Really helpful, friendly and engaging and has opened my eyes up to the inequalities we face in our society. Has made my final year great so far and always there to offer support; a credit to the university and a role model and inspiration to all.

I developed the 3D Pedagogy workshop in 2018 in full consultation with the students' union and had several meetings, in 2018/19, with the Student Vice President for Education Lenrick Greaves, who gave his full endorsement to the 3D Pedagogy Framework. At the 2018 BU Students' Union BME (Black and Minority Ethnic) Awards, I received the first ever Staff Member of the Year Award. Media Inequality also received written praise from the External Examiner. At the end of the 2018/19 academic year I applied for promotion, listing education as a major area. I was hopeful after being shortlisted, but when my application was unsuccessful I lodged an appeal. Imagine my surprise on receiving a letter from the Joint Chair of the Independent Pay Promotion and Progression Panel advising me my appeal was denied, stating: 'Having reviewed your application against the Academic Career Framework, my view is that you do not evidence an established research profile and trajectory, and with education it is not clear what outcomes/impact you have achieved.' I was profoundly disappointed, saddened and frustrated that my contributions and achievements had been completely disregarded. I earnestly believed there had been progress in the years since hooks (1994: 204) warned that critical pedagogy 'is not the intellectual work that most folks think is hip and cool', that 'teachers are more rewarded when we do not teach against the grain. The choice to work against the grain, to challenge the status quo, often has negative consequences' (hooks, 1994: 203).

Negative consequences of engaged pedagogy

Devotion to teaching and pedagogy is rarely rewarded in academia. The time and effort involved in developing, delivering and evaluating critical pedagogy means sacrificing time spent on pursuing research topics deemed important to the faculty regime – and race falls firmly outside that sphere of significance, which is determined by predominantly White male and female academics. Nonetheless, like hooks (1994: 202) I believe 'engaged pedagogy has been essential to my development as an intellectual' and that it 'is an expression of political activism'. However, the challenges that a commitment to engaged pedagogy present go beyond the curtailing of career progression. Not only is it 'taxing to the spirit' (hooks, 1994: 202) but sometimes resistance comes from the very constituents that you strive so hard for. In my chapter in IT1 on being objectified and dehumanized as a Black female academic, I reflect on how objectification and dehumanization occur when we are deemed 'not to conform to the dominant, normative conception of an academic, which is a status reserved for White men primarily, but also for White women' (Gabriel and Tate, 2017: 26).

I share hooks's (1994: 9) experience of students sometimes rebelling against transformative pedagogy with 'rigid resistance', which adds to the emotional toil of teaching as a Black female academic. This manifests in various ways, sometimes through unacceptable confrontational behaviour by students in the classroom. On one occasion when I experienced this in a politics class, I brought the issue to the programme leader formally, who agreed that an apology was called for. However, the student apologized to her, but never to me! On another occasion with a different politics cohort who were overall a delight to teach, a small group of right-wing students went to the White, male head of department and complained about my teaching style and abilities. Several of the students in that cohort came to me personally to disassociate themselves from the actions of their fellow classmates, assuring me they enjoyed my classes immensely, and this was affirmed by one of the student representatives for the course. However, I was still deeply saddened both by the experience and the lack of counselling or support from senior faculty staff who were either ignorant of or indifferent to the raced and gendered micro-aggressions we sometimes endure as Black female lecturers. I have resigned myself to the realization that engendering critical thinking in students is a challenge that comes with the territory: 'Any classroom that employs a holistic model of learning will also be a place where teachers grow, and are empowered by the process. That empowerment cannot happen if we refuse to be vulnerable while encouraging students to take risks' (hooks, 1994: 21). I believe that as Black female academics we are more likely to be challenged and confronted by students whom we teach, though paradoxically this is an indicator of the transformation we seek:

> The exciting aspect of creating a classroom community where there is respect for individual voices is that there is infinitely more feedback because students do feel free to talk – and talk back... shifting paradigms or sharing knowledge in new ways challenges; it takes time for students to experience that challenge as positive. (hooks, 1994: 42)

hooks asserts that engaged pedagogy is not merely about teaching to deepen student engagement but to facilitate our wellbeing as teachers: 'teachers must be actively committed to a process of self-actualization that promotes their own wellbeing if they are to teach in a manner that empowers students' (hooks, 1994: 15). As someone who considers herself both a critical leader and scholar-activist, I have always maintained that I cannot empower others if I am not empowered myself. I have therefore found it essential to create strategies for self-empowerment when others seek to constrain, derogate or oppress me. My preferred method is resistance poetry, through which I critically reflect on and theorize my raced and gendered experiences of inequality. This poem I wrote called 'Whiteness and Privilege Inside the Ivory Tower' is a perfect example:

> It's so unjust that because of my race,
> Whiteness and privilege pollute my space,
> A space in which I strive to promote equality and liberation,
> To challenge oppression and domination,
> But instead whiteness and privilege pollute my space,
> I am violated, disrespected and lied to my face,
> It threatens my sanity when whiteness and privilege deny my
>   humanity,
> Though a proud, strong woman I stand, this institutional space is
>   toxic and sour,
> Inside the ivory tower.
>
> Gabriel, 2017

Conclusion

In this chapter I have reflected on my journey as a scholar-activist and my endeavours to drive transformation in teaching and learning through my development of the 3D Pedagogy Framework. My objectives are both to enhance the learning experience and outcomes of students of colour and to engender agency and critical consciousness in all my students in the hope of them becoming agents of change in employment and the wider society. My analysis of assessment outcomes for the three years I taught Media Inequality shows that students of colour perform marginally better than White students, though the difference is less than one percentage point. This suggests that 3D Pedagogy has the capability of building equity so that all students achieve academic outcomes that utilize their full potential. As highlighted in this chapter, putting one's head above the parapet in this manner comes with risks and may result in negative consequences, both in terms of unfulfilled career ambitions and, on occasion, resistance to change by students.

I initially developed the 3D Pedagogy Framework as a mechanism for enhancing my own teaching practice and later recognized its potential for wider transformation across the HE sector. This led to my development of the 3D Pedagogy Workshop for lecturers and teaching staff. Since it evolved from consultancy activities, my preferred dissemination for it is through consultancy. I have therefore been delivering the 3D Pedagogy Workshop in this manner, not just in media faculties but also in law, sports and management, as I developed 3D Pedagogy as a generic framework that can be contextualized to different disciplines.

Ironically, I have twice been granted internal funding from my university to deliver my workshop across the entire institution as a potential solution to the attainment gap. On both occasions I was unable to do so due to a heavy workload from the competing responsibility of co-leading the Race Equality Charter Self-Assessment Team for three years. Consequently, funding was withdrawn as it was not spent within the prescribed time limit. Having stepped down from that role and had time to reflect critically, I am relieved that my 3D Pedagogy Framework will not be utilized as an institutional tool to be operationalized within an increasingly marketized, bureaucratized environment. Under such conditions, social justice is not the primary driver for institution-wide adoption of emancipatory pedagogies (which tend to lose their criticality when operationalized at a macro level). I am determined that my 3D Pedagogy Framework remains a holistic model of inclusive teaching and learning practice and catalyst for change:

> The academy is not paradise. But learning is a place where paradise can be created. The classroom, with all its limitations remains a location of possibility. In that field of possibility we have the opportunity to labor for freedom, to demand of ourselves and our comrades an openness of mind and heart that allows us to face reality even as we collectively imagine ways to move beyond boundaries, to transgress. This is education as the practice of freedom. (hooks, 1994: 207)

References

Aldridge, D.P. (2000) 'On race and culture: Beyond Afrocentrism, Eurocentrism to cultural democracy'. *Sociological Focus*, 33 (1), 95–107.

Bell, L.A. (2007) 'Theoretical Foundations for Social Justice Education'. In Adams, M., Bell, L.A. and Griffin, P. (eds) *Teaching for Diversity and Social Justice*. London: Routledge, 1–14.

Blay, Y.A. (2008) 'All the "Africans" are men, all the "Sistas" are "American," but some of us resist: Realizing African feminism(s) as an Africological research methodology'. *Journal of Pan African Studies*, 2 (2), 58–73.

Darder, A. (1994) 'Institutional research as a tool for cultural democracy'. *New Directions for Institutional Research*, 81, 21–34.

Gabriel, D. (2016) 'Race, racism and resistance in British academia'. In Fereidooni, K. and El, M. (eds) *A Critical Study of (Trans) National Racism: Interdependence of racist phenomenon and resistance forms*. Wiesbaden: Springer, 493–505.

Gabriel, D. (2017) 'Whiteness and privilege inside the ivory tower'. Online. https://blackbritishacademics.co.uk/2017/10/27/whiteness-and-privilege-inside-the-ivory-tower/ (accessed 12 January 2020).

Gabriel, D. (2018) 'Pedagogies of social justice and cultural democracy in media higher education'. *Media Education Research Journal* (8.1), 35–48.

Gabriel, D. and Tate, S.A. (eds) (2017) *Inside the Ivory Tower: Narratives of women of colour surviving and thriving in British academia.* London: Trentham Books.

Hill Collins, P. (1990) *Black Feminist Thought: Knowledge, consciousness and the politics of empowerment.* New York: Unwin Hyman.

hooks, b. (1994) *Teaching to Transgress: Education as the practice of freedom.* London: Routledge.

Hurtado, S. and Carter, D.F. (1997) 'Effects of college transition and perceptions of the campus racial climate on Latino college students' sense of belonging'. *Sociology of Education* (70) 4, 324–45.

Jackson, L. (2008) 'Dialogic pedagogy for social justice: A critical examination'. *Studies in Philosophy and Education*, 27 (2–3), 137–48.

Mighty, E.J. (2001) 'Teaching For inclusion: The challenges and opportunities of diversity in the classroom'. *Focus on University Teaching and Learning*, 11 (1), 1–8.

Mthethwa-Sommers, S. (2014) 'What is social justice education?' In Sommers, S. (ed.) *Narratives of Social Justice Educators.* New York: Springer International Publishing, 7–23.

Munshi, D. and Edwards, L. (2011) 'Understanding "race" in/and public relations: Where do we start and where should we go?' *Journal of Public Relations Research*, 23 (4), 349–67.

Scheurich, J.J. and Young, M.D. (1997) 'Coloring epistemologies: Are our research epistemologies racially biased?' *Educational Researcher*, 26 (4), 4–16.

Walsh, C. (2012) '"Other" knowledges, "other" critiques: Reflections on the politics and practices of philosophy and decoloniality in the "other" America'. *Transmodernity*, 1 (3), 11–27.

Chapter 2

Building the anti-racist classroom: How the collective makes the radical possible

Deborah N. Brewis, Sadhvi Dar,
Angela Martinez Dy, Helena Liu,
Udeni Salmon on behalf of Building the
Anti-Racist Classroom (BARC) collective

> 'Without community there is no liberation… But community must not
> mean a shedding of our differences, nor the pathetic pretense that these
> differences do not exist.' (Lorde, 2003)

Introduction

Building the Anti-Racist Classroom (BARC) is an international collective of five women of colour scholars working in the field of business and management. Our aims are to promote and facilitate anti-racist, feminist community-building that bridges university stakeholder groups including students, academics and professional services staff. These aims have been developed in response to intensifying individualism and competition among these groups that have further entrenched White patriarchal power structures governing Black women's and women of colour's capacity to flourish in academia. As such, our work engages with racism within our academic field and how it manifests in our working conditions. We have organized our ways of working with one another and of engaging others, informed by the prior experiences, knowledge of collective work and skills we each bring, but without a normative vision for what our anti-racist collective should and will become. We take inspiration from the rich narratives included in Gabriel and Tate (2017) that affected us and our politics at the time we were forming political relations with each other and dreaming about what we must do in order to survive in our academic discipline and respective places of work.

Writing this case study has offered us an opportunity to begin charting a narrative of why and how we came to organize together. It is both a reflection of BARC's organizing principles and an exploration of our differentiated struggles within and against the White academy. The invitation to write this case study offered an opportunity for us to gather together our reflections in one place; to articulate to one another – and now to you – our journeys, hopes and fears; to know our collective more intimately. This chapter marks our first effort to narrate how a certain set of struggles were brought to the surface at a particular moment and how that led us to make commitments to each other and to act on commitments to our communities of colour whose demands for liberation have been largely silenced or ignored by business schools and their scholarship.

Our own differences are both challenging and generative; they must, as Lorde cautions, inform the aims of liberation. When accounting for BARC, we must also be vigilant of when and how systems of power and privilege obscure us from our aims. Differences between marginalized communities can be readily mobilized to disassemble solidarity and therefore a necessary part of organizing collectively is to acknowledge and take seriously the fact that power struggles, misogyny, anti-Blackness, ableism, homophobia, transphobia, Islamophobia and other forms of oppressive politics also exist among communities of colour. To be a collective is to refuse the forces that would see us driven apart entirely by these differences and to nourish those bonds that bring us together. Through working in and with alterity, we can be led by the needs of those who are least likely to make any gains in an environment where resources are scarce (Crenshaw, 1989; Bassel and Emejulu, 2018).

Bridging narratives: Commonalities and differences among the collective

Sadhvi Dar

I had no intention of being an academic. My childhood was spent daydreaming about becoming a poet, an artist, a dancer. I dreamed this as a second-generation Indian immigrant girl, born to a Kashmiri Pandit family and living among extensive and caring Muslim Pakistani and Sikh Punjabi communities in Harrow. I was born into a multi-generational household with paternal grandparents, parents and two other siblings. My elders filled the home with the sounds of old Indian vinyls, with food made according to ancient recipes and with the reverberating insistence of speaking our family's language: a mixture of Hindi and Urdu. Both my grandparents were politically engaged and they kept our regional histories alive by telling and re-telling familial narratives, stories about the liberation movement and the immense destruction, poverty and violence of British, then communal, violence. This knowledge became the foundation of my politics and the framework from which I understood the context of my existence and the experiences of racism I encountered while growing up in Harrow, Middlesex.

When I graduated, I left the UK to spend a year in Delhi. I worked alongside gay, lesbian, hijra, trans activists and then later with an international development agency. Encouraged by a White woman ethnographer in India, I applied to Cambridge's Business School to do a PhD in NGO management. I got in. I felt confused. I suffered alienation in an institution that is relentlessly classist, chauvinist and White. This is not what I wanted, nor what I had bargained for. I left for India again, this time to carry out my fieldwork. The experience revitalized and grounded me. I returned to Cambridge and completed my studies after which I looked for a way out. I didn't find one. I was overqualified to do an office job; I was too Brown to do a policy-level job. A three-month teaching post came up at an East London university and I applied. Ten years later, I was still there, working as a lecturer.

During those ten years I encountered the insidious violence of White power that was exercised at every turn of my career and across multiple spaces: conferences, workshops, lecture theatres, staff meetings and appraisals. Access to my ancestral history and language meant I resisted the internalization of racist logics and battled to keep the truth of my precarity conscious and awake. At the same time, and in the form of an explicit rebuttal of these conditions, I saw people of colour organizing. I looked to South Africa's student protests (Rhodes Must Fall), then to the American Black Lives Matter movement; Black scholars at UCL organized around the demand: Why is my curriculum White? Something seemed possible in ways that it didn't seem before. After a four-year hiatus from academic conferences, I attended the 2017 Critical Management Studies Conference. It was there that I met a group of women whom I had not encountered before and whose insistence to thrive as women of colour despite the whiteness of business management blew me away.

Helena Liu

I had no intention of being an activist. Growing up the only child of Chinese migrants in Australia who left the Tiananmen Square massacre behind in 1991, I kept my head down and played my part as the model minority. Throughout my adolescence I would vehemently deny the existence of racism, lying to others and myself that we would all be safe. I never found my safety. I entered a sandstone university overrun with anti-Asian sentiment against the predominantly Chinese and Vietnamese international students who allegedly stole their enrolments from more deserving White Australian students. 'Are you one of us or one of them?' The hostile glares from my fellow local students demanded I demonstrate my allegiance. 'Howya doin mate?' I would reply, making my fealty clear. White students and teachers would relax, smile, call on me more in class and my assignments were returned with higher grades. Correct answer, I thought.

In part, I chose leadership as my area of research for my PhD because it seemed the furthest away from the stereotypically quantitative disciplines of accounting and finance that someone like me was expected to pursue. It was two years after my graduation when I turned to anti-racism as an intellectual tradition and political movement. The more I studied, the lighter I felt, as if I was given the licence and the language to speak truth to my pain. When I heard decolonial feminists including Sadhvi Dar were running a meeting for like-minded scholars on the final day of the 2017 Critical Management Studies Conference, I joined the diverse group of co-conspirators, bringing along a box of chocolates, and met women who later became my BARC sisters. Their strength has made me stronger and their courage made me more courageous. I no longer deny my own pain, my own rage, and through this truth I have found solidarity, hope and love.

Angela Martinez Dy

I am a conflicted business management scholar. A Filipina American poet, teaching artist and community organizer by background, with a double major first degree in mathematics and creative writing. I took an MSc in entrepreneurship primarily as a one-year retreat from the burnout I experienced as the founder-director of a youth arts organization in Seattle in my late teens and early 20s. My excellence in English language educational settings propelled me to the top of the class and a PhD studentship in digital entrepreneurship, followed by a permanent post as an entrepreneurship lecturer. While I love the relative autonomy and benefit from the privilege of academic life, I miss the brilliant, brave, socially minded and creative communities I come from. These are the Black, Indigenous and people of colour (BIPOC) artists and activists, especially queer, trans and non-binary folk, alongside radical White allies who created the conditions and settings that gave rise to my political consciousness in Seattle, Washington, Duwamish land, at the turn of the twenty-first century.

The formation of the Decolonizing Alliance in response to the marginalization of women and gender scholars, Global South scholars and scholars of disability at the 2017 Critical Management Studies Conference was a natural outcropping of my instinct to organize. The meeting brought together most of the cadre of women who now constitute BARC, a vehicle by which to use the substantial platform of the profoundly White, patriarchal and pro-capitalist business management discipline to advance the collectivist, anti-racist, intersectional feminist politics and practices that have been the foundation for any liberation I have ever felt in my lifetime.

Deborah N. Brewis

I have found it hard to write this section on who I am and what brought me to BARC. I have started and restarted it, procrastinated a little by editing other parts. My feelings about my identity are characterized by an in-betweeness, a discomfort and longing. They've always been there but for a long time I did what I could to not think about them or to attribute them elsewhere, their target unclear, or too frightening. I am a mixed-race woman, with both Chinese and Welsh families living in the UK. My Chinese family migrated from Vietnam in the wake of the war. I have been closer to members of my Chinese family throughout my life and witnessed their treatment as outsiders as I grew up: sometimes benevolently, sometimes as curiosities, sometimes with suspicion, sometimes with distaste. These are simultaneously not my stories to tell, yet so fundamental to who I am that looking back I see that they have informed everything I have done.

I struggle to know how I appear to others. Veiled questions about my heritage have come and gone in different periods of my life as my face has changed and the contexts in which I work and live have shifted. I've been learning recently that many see me as non-White but do not say so. I was only really subject to racializing taunts as a child; young, safe, and favoured enough by teachers to fend off a few individuals in the schoolyard myself. I have benefited from a large degree of privilege in this and in other things my upbringing encouraged me to explore and pursue my passions. It is this instinct to follow a feeling of embodied energizing connection that led me to surround myself with people who I respect, admire and care for; who nourish something in me I could not articulate. To commit to them, to commit to our shared causes, to build community, to do differently. As I have moved through the academic disciplines from arts and humanities to social sciences and to management and organization, I have thankfully trusted my feet, which have stepped closer and closer towards those ideas and people who seek to see, to speak and to act against the fundamental schisms and violence of the world. Becoming part of BARC and allowing it to transform me has been a most unexpected and most natural part of my journey.

Udeni Salmon

I am a cis-gender, non-White, Sri Lankan, English, British, Buddhist, middle-class woman. I am a daughter, sister, aunt and wife. In my 20s and 30s I achieved an MSc in computation, an MA in English and Russian and an MBA. I came back to academia to study for a PhD in my mid-40s, having uneasily pursued a career in the private, public and voluntary sectors. I naively thought that academia would welcome my blend of industry experience and intellectual curiosity. Instead I found an insular, snobbish world that was dominated by middle-class, English, White men and women. As a PhD student in the Business School I found it hard to find friends and build intellectual networks. Academics and students found my age, my race, my gender and my work experience threatening. Towards the end of my PhD I organized a series of lectures on race and invited Deborah Gabriel to launch *Inside the Ivory Tower*. Gabriel's principled insistence on all the authors attending was my first experience of collective organizing in the academy. Inspired by her, I seized on the invitation to join BARC. For me, BARC was born from a shared sense of rage: how universities, which should be a vehicle for social and racial justice, had been co-opted by the White, male, straight, middle-class majority. BARC was our response to that rage: we aim to build a better future.

What's White about business management?

When women of colour forge alliances with one another and commit to putting each other's bodies, power and knowledge at the centre of all that we do, we are drawing on a wisdom nurtured by our foremothers and a capacity that has been built by them over generations (Moraga and Anzaldúa, 1983). We organize as a collective for each other and with each other in mind: we acknowledge, as Lorde (2003) contends, that community is a radical concept, for it negates the notion that the individual is paramount. The existence of the collective rejects too the notion that solidarity can be achieved while marginalized communities are splintered and turned away from one another. This splintering has been the result of forces such as White feminism, as well as anti-Blackness among communities of colour, all of which higher education management utilizes to serve its own ends. At the same time, our own struggles are testimony that all communities are internally differentiated and our collective liberation depends on being continually self-reflexive and open to critique, vulnerable with one another and seeking learning.

Seeking learning happens in a particular context. Today there are more than 120 UK universities (out of 150 or so) that offer students an education in business and management. It is a subject area that attracts the third-highest proportion of British undergraduate students of colour, only after medicine and law (UUK, 2015; see also Dar, 2018). While some critics focus on the under-representation of academics of colour in business schools (HESA, 2019), the more meaningful question for us is, *how does our field enshrine and perpetuate White power?* The answer may only partially be found in numerical representation. The modern evolution of business schools as university departments has meant the funding structure of a significant proportion of the business and management discipline is associated with extra-academic bodies such as Big Business, high-net-worth individuals or corporate partnerships. Such relations of (White) capital must inevitably shape governance structures that inform how decisions are made about the kinds of academics that are valued, research that is facilitated and the students this attracts. As such, the largely anti-intellectual and pro-profit orientation of business school objectives marginalizes critical voices that challenge dominant White, patriarchal, capitalist forms of economic organization.

Analyses of racial inequalities within business and management student and academic groups are sparse and, in particular, contributions authored by students of colour and academics of colour (e.g. Molisa, 2010; Ruggunnan, 2016; Love *et al.*, 2018; Liu, 2018b, 2019; Dar, 2019; BreakThrough! 2018). While some of these contributions are led by our own collective's members and signify clear demands that White power structures acknowledge their role in the oppression of people of colour, there is an overwhelming silence and inertia in relation to how business and management privileges White people and White knowledge. As in other academic fields among the broadly termed social sciences or humanities, a post-race myth is sustained about the state of equality in Europe, North America (Lentin and Titley, 2011) and Australia. This has meant that when experiences of racist bullying, harassment or injustice are brought to the attention of a manager or another authority figure, the facts can end up being reframed by management as individual, unsubstantiated opinions. These denials have contributed to us not only experiencing painful levels of exclusion, alienation and self-doubt, but also to our need to speak our truths as a collective of non-Black, predominantly queer-identified, women of colour.

In spite of the dominance of White power over all aspects of business school governance, scholars from within the field have written about the epistemic violence of business studies that devalues and silences knowledge from the Global South and people of colour (see, for example, Nkomo, 1992; Ibarra-Colado, 2001, 2006; Osuri and Banerjee, 2003; Cooke, 2003; Guedes and Faria, 2010; Gantman *et al.*, 2015). While these contributions have provided the discipline with rich and in-depth counter-logics, the translation of these debates into tangible pedagogic practice remains stubbornly marginal. For example, these critical authors of colour are rarely featured in taught modules and curricula and are also obscured in mainstream understandings about international management and global business. This is not something new or phenomenal about the present conditions under which we teach, learn and research; however, there is a palpable urgency to correct these epistemic inequalities, as our explicitly racist and anti-immigrant times necessitate incisive anti-racist critique and alternative models for organizing and equitizing (Liu *et al.*, 2020; Johnson *et al.*, 2018).

While the historical exclusion of Black women and women of colour from academic scholarship cannot be ignored (Gabriel and Tate, 2017), the relatively recent marketization of British higher education has intensified these exclusions and undermined the potential for critique within our scholarly fields and pedagogical practices. The political economy of higher education has become increasingly deregulated, leading to a competitive environment where scholars compete for publications in high-ranking journals, internal and external research funding, postgraduate teaching, teaching specialism-based modules, recruiting PhD students and, in some universities, for academic bonuses.

An example of this marketization is the British Research Excellence Framework (REF) – a market instrument that awards higher education institutions with funding based on their ranking along a scale of 'excellence'. The scale aggregates individual academics' 'value' based on an evaluation of their capacity to publish research and lead a research field. The criteria for excellence are drawn up by mostly White male professors and the methodology has been criticized for its gendered and racialized exclusionism (Stern, 2016). Critique of these structures is almost impossible because when knowledge is commodified its value is tethered to its supposedly value-free apolitical credentials (Osuri, 2007). Furthermore, this competition takes place in classist, racist and sexist structures in which power is maintained among predominantly middle- to upper-class White male academics over all forms of decision-making, strategic management and governance of influential journals, promotion panels, diversity initiatives and university management. When women of colour demand inclusion in higher education, the struggle is not only against whiteness, patriarchy or classism but is an explicit rebuttal of the interlocking power structures that manage every aspect of their academic careers.

The solidaristic bonds woven among women of colour are not so much the products of any deliberate project but are quite often the results of ad hoc struggles for survival. For BARC, we did not set out to mimic the prevailing model of organizations with explicit aims, strategies, functions, reporting lines and key performance indicators. In the next section, we recount the organic course of connection and kinship that brought us together and BARC into being.

The decolonizing alliance: Invoking community, demanding inclusion

In Liverpool in the summer of 2017, a group of management and organization scholars organized an impromptu anti-racist decolonizing workshop on the final day of the International Critical Management Studies conference. The workshop was a joint effort among Jenny Rodriguez, Marcela Mandiola, Sadhvi Dar, Gregorio Perez and Alex Faria, who were moved to make an intervention after a series of instances and events over the previous few days had left them feeling frustrated by the conference's ignorance of White power and privilege in business management, alongside its disturbing silence on Brexit, Trump and anti-migrant violence. The workshop was promoted by the organizing academics via word of mouth, targeting doctoral students of colour in particular, and it galvanized a diverse group comprising students, early career researchers and more senior faculty.

Key to organizing the space was the levelling work that set the tone of how participants could be themselves in the space and feel safe enough to voice their opinions. Sadhvi made a circle of chairs and put bottles of water and cups in the centre. Jenny kept the door ajar, using a chair as a doorstop. The organizers waited for participants, expecting around 12 or perhaps 15 people to show up, but the circle unexpectedly grew to accommodate 40. Marcela welcomed everyone to the workshop, Sadhvi described why it had been set up and Jenny presented her paper 'Why is my curriculum so White?' to spark discussion. What followed was an outpouring from workshop participants, their sentiments ranging from anger and frustration to solidaristic support. Angela, Afroz and Deborah unfurled a large banner in the centre of the circle that had become a site for protest during the conference, and surrounding participants began to suggest additions. These discussions highlighted the need to turn talking-points towards action, and by the end of the two-hour session the group had collectively inaugurated themselves as the Decolonizing Alliance (DA).

The aims of DA were uncomplicated: to show up to support each other, to recognize each other's marginalization, to develop an inclusive community for research and activism. Of these 40 participants, Angela Martinez Dy, Deborah Brewis, Afroz Zain Algiers, Helena Liu, Vick Virtu, Fahreen Alamgir, Alessia Contu and Rafael Alcadipani were among the notable contributors. A JiscMail list, Google Drive and Facebook community page were set up to pool resources, open communication channels and lay down the technological infrastructure around which an emerging trans-global community could organize. The group was hailed as a significant breakthrough in the discipline's discourse and practice (Contu, 2018, 2019), yet its formation was to have ripple effects that had value beyond any perceived utility or intellectual contribution.

BARC: An anti-racist collective in the making

The support work that had been laid down as an infrastructure for the Alliance led to the solidifying of some critical friendships within the DA community. In the early exchanges during what was to become the formation of BARC, five of us agreed to collaborate on a workshop-funding application without realizing that we were conceiving a collective and a community. Organizing principles were not laid down at first. Instead, we shared practice through suggestions and negotiated ways of working. Organically, we began to organize as a collective while working out what that meant for us in the context of our practice: acknowledging labour (including emotional labour); resisting individualizing; and demanding a work ethic that acknowledges when and how women can work or contribute. Changes to the organizing membership and ways of working were made and continue to be made so that the work does not become overwhelming vis-à-vis personal and professional commitments.

When the funding was awarded, we developed the inaugural BARC workshop at Queen Mary University of London in October 2018. The workshop seemed like an ignition switch that had zoned in on a painful and pressing gap in the higher education sector: working towards Black and communities' of colour liberation. In order to work for liberation, we first identify diversity management initiatives as false liberation, and worse still as a management technique that co-opts radical voices in higher education only to manipulate them on their own terms. Initiatives such as unconscious bias training (Tate and Page, 2018), equality, diversity and inclusion committees (Ahmed, 2012), 'networking opportunities' (BreakThrough!, 2018), Athena Swan (Tzanakou and Pearce, 2019), the Race Equality Charter, ethnic monitoring (Kim and Ng, 2019) and diversity reporting (Ahmed, 2007) receive substantial university funding based on the belief that these practices address racial and gendered inequalities. However, as studies have consistently shown, these initiatives have changed very little in organizations, and power remains concentrated within White, male networks.

For BARC to move away from these failures, two things are emphasized: we organize ourselves around anti-racist, feminist principles, and organize our workshops with these aims: to a) level power relations among stakeholder groups, b) re-imagine an actively anti-racist learning environment in higher education, c) use reflexive thinking, participative methodologies and discussion to generate ideas to identify the structural and local changes we wish to see and imagine how we might get there. We open BARC meetings with a round of personal check-ins, to fully acknowledge each other as members of families, partners, and human beings who feel pleasure and pain; recognizing before we request labour of each other that we are capable but fallible and constrained. We seek to enact our shared principles through care for our own community, making space for personal lives, to talk over tea, spend time in each other's homes, cook and eat together and even enable time away from the work. We seek to nourish and to uplift one another, to be generous and to sacrifice in defiance of the inward-turned isolation and competitiveness of the neoliberal university that would otherwise appropriate 'decolonizing', or even 'activism', for instrumental and individual ends (Dar *et al.*, 2018). Fundamental to our relational interactions is an explicit self-reflexivity that is not permitted or typically possible in the marketized White masculinist academy, an unfamiliar but freeing practice in which we intentionally continue to engage as it deepens and transforms our relationships.

The White masculinist discipline of business and management is one in which Black scholars and scholars of colour continue to struggle for recognition as fully human. In these margins we are more than colleagues, for the degree to which we must trust and offer ourselves requires it. Anti-racist relationships are built through organizing together and showing up: standing meetings, digital collaborations, workshops, discussions, writing and pedagogy to facilitate what we need most of all to sustain us – continual dialogue and mutual giving to the work and to each other. We locate other anti-racist scholar-activists at conferences, in journal articles and on social media; we tentatively reach out to see if we speak a common language. We aim to foster truly collaborative relationships that enable us to be heard from the margins.

Unlike most work in the academy, our workshops are organized as much as possible on our own terms as women of colour. The difference this makes in the tone and outcomes of our interventions is profound. We set guidelines for a principled space in which an ontology of the world where race is constructed but racism is real is fundamental. In this space, the experiences of marginalization and oppression explained by people of colour are not to be questioned but believed. We have witnessed tears of relief when participants of colour realize that they are truly seen. We ask for positive affirmation of these principles and invite those who cannot subscribe to them to leave, so that they do not inhibit the work we have come to do. No one has left yet, although some may find the work difficult and demanding.

Our workshops feature lectures and panel discussions with predominantly women of colour keynotes, combined with active learning methods, such as bespoke games, drawing, body mapping, and writing exercises. We strive to meet those in the room where they are at, make visible the labour and struggles of people of colour, and model examples of supportive, non-hierarchical leadership and privilege-checking. We feed and fund people, to show care and enable them to contribute, and we have learned over time to remember to make space to breathe. Our efforts build primarily upon the work of people of colour and women, and we always acknowledge our sources. We also admit what we don't know or understand and when we are pushed to our intellectual limit or comfort-zone edge with the stated intention to seek advice, return soon and continue stretching ourselves as we invite our workshop participants to do the same.

We especially relish the work we do with students and professional services staff of colour, lending our position, privilege and platforms to those whose experiences are often made invisible by institutional racism. In such partnerships we are mindful to not dominate discussions and we aim to provide methodologies, rather than frameworks or toolkits, for developing interventions. Underpinning our methodological approach are artistic frameworks that centre affect and relationality instead of logocentrism. We use zine-making, board games, poetry, music and theatre to challenge European-imperial knowledge production. These methodologies are not new in themselves, but we have found that they function as a powerful reminder to claim our voice and make our collective demands heard by the White elites and institutions who would rather turn away in denial.

The community that emerged around the 2018 workshop called out for further interventions. We quickly became inundated with commissions to deliver similar workshops across the UK in our unusual capacity as scholar-activists. While most offers for commission represented tantalizing possibilities, a sense of dread surfaced with others. After a lengthy conversation about the hows and whos of a prospective event, a moment of frankness with one another broke through in which we realized that our hesitations and resultant sufferings were arising from a wariness of White patronage, which continually risks the appropriation of our knowledge and bodies in service of White ignorance (Mills, 2007). We made a choice then to be circumspect about commissions that wanted us to scale up our workshops, determine our audiences, set out or restrict our direction and agility as a collective. As a result, we have sharpened our focus instead on activities that would serve our efforts in community-building with and for people of colour and radical anti-racist work led by Black students and students of colour.

The radical heart of anti-racist feminisms

Udeni Salmon

My hopes, dreams and ambitions for BARC are limitless. The sheer joy of writing, talking, planning and teaching with BARC is irresistible. We all feel that joy, no matter how hard it is to commit to BARC in the face of our responsibilities to full-time jobs, families and friendships. Accordingly, I have hope that our work is built on solid foundations. We work with and through the individual, on a human scale. While our work is still rooted in the individual, we will ultimately transform the structure of the White-dominated academy. We continue to plan, debate, discuss and dream. The future of our collective endeavour will evolve as we continue to change and grow. We hope that this chapter has reassured others who are perhaps in a similarly lonely place to that in which we found ourselves. Collective organizing in the academy is not only possible but thriving.

Deborah N. Brewis

My hope for BARC is that in our time together we are able to act effectively from the odd and privileged position of scholar-activists. That both our scholarship and outreach contribute in a meaningful way to the building of a community that will generate ideas, connections and possibilities that we cannot each foresee on our own. I want us to continue to find the ways that we uniquely can act and to share; to use the knowledge, capacities and resources that we can leverage. I hope for us to play a part in spreading not only consciousness and strategy but also care, validation and joy. My vision is for a world with far less violence in it; a world without oppression as its core organizing principle. I hope that together and as part of other movements we are able to serve this work long enough to see changes that move us towards this future.

Angela Martinez Dy

I dream that we can make BARC a microcosm of the kind of world we wish to inhabit. The concept of fractals introduced in adrienne maree brown's book Emergent Strategy (2017) reminds us that the large reflects the small. If we, small as we are, can iron out ways of working collectively that are loving, honest, generous and generative, informed by both fact and feeling, allow for learning from failure and are sustainable as long as they are fit for purpose, then this is revolutionary in itself. As we apply our shared analyses, teach and shape change (brown, 2017) around us, we can model for ourselves what is possible, which is so necessary in the absence of clear signposts to a fairer and more just future. I have lived through the birth and death of radical collectives of colour irreparably wounded by internal power struggles, lack of accountability, drama, secrecy and shame. I believe these collapses have occurred because of inexperience plus the inverse of the fractal principle – the small also reflects the large. Though in this world we are not taught to work and play well non-hierarchically, if we ourselves cannot do it, it is hypocrisy to expect others to do so.

At the same time, we should not strive for a meaningless perfection, but rather continually stretch ourselves closer to what we wish to become. It is our task as twenty-first-century activists to learn from past mistakes, focus on our aims and resist the programming that teaches us that we must be in competition for power, scarce resources and the spotlight. The more we support each other and pull our own weight to the extent that we are able – our knowledge, strength and capacity growing all the while – the greater we and our work will be and the effects seen and felt accordingly.

Helena Liu

I think back sometimes to the young woman I was, broken by bitter resentment that I could not be White enough to fit into the academy. Her fury comes out now when, as an established academic, I'm asked to make some special accommodation for privileged White students, who complain to me of how 'tired' they are of working with students of colour in their courses. I cannot sympathize with their entitlement expectation that authority figures exist to make their lives more comfortable. Instead, my gaze will wander to the students of colour working behind them, in those moments of recognition when they know they are being constructed as the 'problem' and when the axes of power in institutions are being bent away from their needs and interests, their safety and wellbeing.

BARC has been a source of healing and nourishment for me and I hope that as we are restored as academics of colour, our energies may be doubled towards ameliorating the lives of those most vulnerable in our community. I want to be there for students of colour. I also want to be there for other staff of colour, particularly the administrators and precarious workers whose suffering is often more acute and yet stifled without these vital platforms for expression. Knowing that racism does not operate without the simultaneous enforcement of sexism, heteronormativity, ableism, capitalism and imperialism, the future of our politics is about building solidarity with other marginalized communities and their resistive struggles and, together, build a feminist, queer, socialist, decolonial future.

Sadhvi Dar

During a wrap-up session at a student-organized conference at the University of Kent, Azeezat Johnson told the audience that sometimes a collective has a timely purpose. Its greatest power may be that it exists for the communities who need it most or that it lays down infrastructure – both ideological and material – that future communities of colour and anti-racist Whites can build around or be nourished by. In December 2019, BARC marked two years of organizing collectively. How we collaboratively engage with White power in the future will depend on the relevance of our individual and collective politics in relation to the changing power structures that determine our position, visibility and capacity to be generative in British academia. This relevance will have everything to do with our capacities to sustain patterns of working in a particular way and very little to do with our capacity for political action. For women of colour to exist in the White academy is to resist the White academy (Emejulu and Sobande, 2019) and we do not need to put our bodies in harm's way on a daily basis for the lofty and unrealistic aims to valiantly overthrow White capitalist patriarchies once and for all. The radical heart of anti-racist work is being exactly who we are while knowing that who we are transgresses the racialized systems of creating value in British higher education (Pow, 2018). We do the work because it is how we sustain our existence in the White academy. We will continue to exist after BARC because the collective has made the radical possible.

References

Ahmed, S. (2007) '"You end up doing the document rather than doing the doing": Diversity, race equality and the politics of documentation'. *Ethnic and Racial Studies*, 30 (4), 590–609.

Ahmed, S. (2012) *On Being Included: Racism and diversity in institutional life.* Durham, NC: Duke University Press.

BreakThrough! (2018) The Bangladeshi Women's Careers Group Report 1. Online. https://breakthroughbangladeshiwomen.files.wordpress.com/2018/11/breakthroughreportfinal.pdf (accessed 12 January 2020).

Bassel, L., and Emejulu, A. (2018). 'Caring subjects: Migrant women and the third sector in England and Scotland'. *Ethnic and Racial Studies*, 41 (1), 36–54.

brown, a.m. (2017) *Emergent Strategy.* Chico, CA: AK Press.

Contu, A. (2018) '"… The point is to change it" – Yes, but in what direction and how? Intellectual activism as a way of "walking the talk" of critical work in business schools'. *Organization*, 25 (2), 282–93.

Contu, A. (2019) 'Conflict and organization studies'. *Organization Studies*, 40 (10), 1445–62.

Cooke, B. (2003) 'The denial of slavery in management studies'. *Journal of Management Studies*, 40 (8), 1895–1918.

Crenshaw, K. (1989) 'Demarginalizing the intersection of race and sex: A black feminist critique of antidiscrimination doctrine, feminist theory and anti-racist politics'. *University of Chicago Legal Forum*, 1 (8), Volume 1989.

Dar, S. (2018) 'Why we need anti-racist Business Schools'. Online. www.leftofbrown.com/single-post/2018/01/07/Why-We-Need-Anti-Racist-Business-Schools (accessed 12 January 2020).

Dar, S. (2019) 'The masque of Blackness: Or, performing assimilation in the white academe'. *Organization*, 26 (3), 432–46.

Dar, S., Martinez Dy, A. and Rodriguez, J.K. (2018) 'Is decolonising the new black?' Online. www.leftofbrown.com/single-post/2018/07/12/Is-decolonising-the-new-black (accessed 12 January 2020).

Emejulu, A. and Sobande, F. (eds) (2019) *To Exist is to Resist: Black feminism in Europe*. London: Pluto Press.

Gabriel, D. and Tate, S.A. (eds) (2017) *Inside the Ivory Tower: Narratives of women of colour thriving and surviving in British academia*. London: Trentham Books.

Gantman, E.R., Yousfi, H., and Alcadipani, R. (2015). 'Challenging Anglo-Saxon dominance in management and organizational knowledge'. *Revista de Administração de Empresas*, 55 (2), 126–9.

Guedes, A. and Faria, A. (2010) 'Bringing the "international" into international management: New challenges'. In Guedes, A. and Faria, A. (eds) *International Management and International Relations: A critical perspective from Latin America*. New York: Routledge, 245–56.

HESA (2019) 'Table 12 – HE academic staff by nationality and cost centre 2014/15 to 2017/18'. Online. www.hesa.ac.uk/data-and-analysis/staff/table-12 (accessed 12 January 2020).

Ibarra-Colado, E. (2001) 'Considering "new formulas" for a "renewed university": The Mexican experience'. *Organization*, 8 (2), 203–17.

Ibarra-Colado, E. (2006) 'Organization studies and epistemic coloniality in Latin America: Thinking otherness from the margins'. *Organization*, 13 (4), 463–88.

Johnson, A., Joseph-Salisbury, R. and Kamunge, B. (eds) (2018) *The Fire Now: Anti-racist scholarship in times of explicit racial violence*. London: Zed Books.

Kim, T. and Ng, W. (2019) 'Ticking the "other" box: Positional identities of East Asian academics in UK universities, internationalisation and diversification'. *Policy Reviews in Higher Education*, 3 (1), 94–119. DOI:10.1080/23322969.2018.1564886 (accessed 12 January 2020).

Lentin, A. and Titley, G. (2011) *The Crises of Multiculturalism: Racism in a neoliberal age*. London: Zed Books.

Liu, H. (2018a) 'My dearest friends of colour'. *M@n@gement*, 21 (3), 1105–6.

Liu, H. (2018b) 'Re-radicalising intersectionality in organization studies'. *ephemera: theory & politics in organization*, 18 (1), 81–101.

Liu, H. (2019) 'An embarrassment of riches: The seduction of postfeminism in the academy'. *Organization*, 26 (1), 20–37.

Liu, H., Dar, S., Brewis, D.N., Martinez Dy, A. (forthcoming, 2020) 'Anti-racism in the age of white supremacy and backlash', Special Issue call for papers, *Equality, Diversity and Inclusion*, closing 31st December 2019. Online. https://tinyurl.com/ycmkkjle

Lorde, A. (2003) 'The master's tools will never dismantle the master's house'. In Lewis, R. and Mills, S. (eds) *Feminist Postcolonial Theory: A reader*. New York: Routledge, 25–7.

Love, T., Finsterwalder, J. and Tombs A. (2018) 'Māori knowledge and consumer tribes'. *MAI Journal: A New Zealand Journal of Indigenous Scholarship*, Special Issue on Whai Rawa: Research for Māori Economies, 7 (1), 44–50.

Mills, C.W. (2007) 'Racial ignorance'. In Sullivan, S. and Tuyana, N. (eds) *Race and Epistemologies of Ignorance*. Albany, NY: SUNY Press, 11–38.

Molisa, P. (2010) 'White business education'. *Critical Perspectives on Accounting*, 21 (6), 525–8.

Moraga, C., and Anzaldúa, G. (1983) *This Bridge Called my Back*. New York: Kitchen Table Women of Color Press.

Nkomo, S.M. (1992) 'The emperor has no clothes: Rewriting "race in organizations"'. *Academy of Management Review*, 17 (3), 487–513.

Osuri G. (2007) 'How to stop worrying about the neoliberal present and start engaging with it'. *Australian Feminist Studies*, 22 (52), 145–7.

Osuri, G. and Banerjee, S.B. (2003) 'Organizing multiple spacetimes in a colonial context: Indigeneity and white Australian nationalism at the Melbourne Museum'. In Linstead, S. (ed.) *Text/Work: Representing organization and organizing representation*. London: Routledge, 148–70.

Pow, K. (2018) '"Be exactly who you are": Black feminism in volatile political realities'. In Johnson, A., Joseph-Salisbury, R. and Kamunge, B. (eds) *The Fire Now: Anti-racist scholarship in times of explicit racial violence*. London: Zed Books, 235–49.

Ruggunan, S.D. (2016) 'Decolonising management studies: A love story'. In 'Critical Management Studies in the South African context', *Acta Commercii*, suppl. 1, 16 (2), a412. Online. http://dx.doi.org/10.4102/ac.v16i2.412 (accessed 12 January 2020).

Stern, N. (2016) *Research Excellence Framework (REF) Review: Building on success and learning from experience*. IND/16/9. Department for Business, Energy & Industrial Strategy.

Tate, S.A. and Page, D. (2018) 'Whiteliness and institutional racism: Hiding behind (un)conscious bias'. *Ethics and Education*, 13 (1), 141–55. Online. DOI: 10.1080/17449642.2018.1428718 (accessed 12 January 2020).

Tzanakou, C. and Pearce, R. (2019) 'Moderate feminism within or against the neoliberal university? The example of Athena SWAN'. *Gender, Work & Organization*, 26 (8), 1191–1211.

UUK (2015) *Patterns and Trends in UK Higher Education*. Online. www.universitiesuk.ac.uk/policy-and-analysis/reports/Documents/2015/patterns-and-trends-2015.pdf (accessed 12 January 2020).

Chapter 3

Addressing barriers to STEM for young Black women using science education and mentoring
Elizabeth Opara

Introduction

Although a Black woman scientist for over thirty years, I was led by a relatively recent experience of isolation to conclude that there are barriers to STEM (science, technology, engineering and mathematics), and specifically to staying and thriving in its disciplines. These barriers need to be dismantled through acts of resistance. In this chapter I explore through my own experiences how the roles of science educator and mentor, which are rooted in an altruistic science identity, can be used to resist White dominance and strangleholds in STEM, and ultimately facilitate the retention and success of Black women in these disciplines.

Three years ago I wrote my contribution to *Inside the Ivory Tower* (Gabriel and Tate, 2017; for convenience referred to as IT1). In my chapter 'The transformation of my science identity' (Opara, 2017: 124) I used a model of science identity developed by Carlone and Johnson (2007: 1187) to describe my transformation from a *recognized* research scientist identity (recognized not only by myself but by my institution) to a disrupted, altruistic science identity (one through which I was forced to accept that I was *not* recognized as a scientist by my institution). I explained that this latter identity is not about achieving ambitions defined by the institution but rather "… a redefinition of whose recognition matters" (Opara, 2017: 130) and using "science in direct service of humanity" (Carlone and Johnson, 2007: 1199).

Three years on, the HE environment remains one in which Black academics in Britain continue to challenge, explore and articulate the nuances of racism in the academy. Clearly, there is a need for profound change (Gabriel, 2018; Bhopal, 2018: 9; Anonymous Academic, 2019). It is in this context that I explore how I use my roles as a science educator and mentor, which are rooted in my altruistic science identity, to address barriers to STEM, specifically of thriving in its disciplines at local level. This chapter aims to offer insights into how Black women who have chosen a career in STEM can identify modes of resistance and develop new strategies that can contribute to dismantling barriers to STEM for young Black women, and ultimately transform the science academy into an inclusive environment.

Context

To present my case study, I first identify what the barriers to STEM are for young Black women and why they exist. Literature suggests that the barriers are possibly cultural and based on how STEM is perceived by certain communities (CaSE, 2014: 43). The paucity of role models is well recognized as a barrier to young Black women studying and pursuing careers in STEM; they see no Black women scientists and engineers so they believe that such careers are not open to them (Jefferson, 2019; WISE, 2014: 17). Familial influence is also reported to be significant. In its report on under-representation in science, technology and engineering, the Women into Science and Engineering (WISE) Campaign reported that Black African and Black Caribbean A-level student interviewees discontinued their studies in STEM subjects, specifically chemistry and physics, in light of perceptions by their families they would have to work twice as hard as other groups to overcome disadvantage (WISE, 2014: 17). Furthermore, Black African A-level students did not perceive that chemistry and physics were worth pursuing to degree level (WISE, 2014: 17). Yet, I believe that at the heart of these barriers is science itself, specifically *how* it is taught and *how* it is practised in the academy, and also the institutions where it is practised. Herein lie the major barriers to be dismantled. However, before examining strategies for resistance, I must reject the notion that science is objective.

In IT1, I discussed how my early beliefs in the objectivity of science were shattered by my experience (Opara, 2017: 124). I had believed that because of its objectivity, science is 'a single, unified front always striving for objective truth...' (Weikart, 2018) and, superficially, science appears to be objective. Those who study science are taught the scientific process by which a person makes an observation from which they develop a hypothesis. This hypothesis is then investigated by carrying out a controlled experiment. You then determine whether the results agree with the hypothesis and, if so, you repeat your experiments and ultimately derive a scientific theory confirming the initial observation. If they disagree, however, you revise the hypothesis and begin again. This process in its pure and unbiased form is objective. Therefore, it is not unreasonable to surmise that science and the scientist are objective. However, the opinions of some scientists are based on prejudiced attitudes that are damaging to people of colour and reflect indifference to race and gender (Sayed, 2016). The controversy concerning James Watson (Winner of the Nobel Prize for Medicine in 1962) is a prime example. He continues to assert that people of African descent are less intelligent than Whites and that the difference is genetic. However, his assertions are not based on scientific process (Rutherford, 2014; Durkin 2019). Scientific research too is not immune to prejudice and bias.

In a letter to the Medical Research Council (MRC) and the Wellcome Trust, Professor David Curtis expressed concerns about Black and minority ethnic groups not gaining from the medical benefits of genetics research because of the 'overwhelming bias towards studying White European populations' (Devlin, 2018). Concerns were expressed that such exclusive research was meaningless and potentially damaging when applied to Black and minority ethnic groups, especially when it was increasingly used in clinical contexts. A chilling example of this is the genetics test to predict risk of schizophrenia, where people of African descent score higher than those of European descent (Curtis, 2018). Professor Curtis stated that the current situation was so acute that 'UK medical science stands at risk of being accused of being institutionally racist' (Devlin, 2018). The chief executive of the MRC responded thus: 'I do not think it is helpful to cast concerns over experimental design as inequalities issues'. In light of the recent push to prioritize diversity and inclusion in STEM by establishment(s) in the UK (British Science Association, n.d) and US regarding research into the human genome – a push led by scientists from under-represented groups (Guglielmi, 2019) – it is ironic and frustrating that the establishment deems it acceptable and reasonable, in 2019, to respond in such a way.

This non-objective, Eurocentric culture predicated by the Whiteness that dominates the science academy is a barrier to STEM because the frequently encountered barriers contribute to the poor retention and limited success of Black women in STEM, particularly in academia. The Campaign for Science and Engineering (CaSE) 2014 reported that Caribbean women made up 8 per cent and Black African women 25 per cent of women studying STEM subjects in 2009/10 (CaSE, 2014: 42). However, such percentages are not reflected in the numbers of Black women science academics in general. One prime example is the number of Black women professors in STEM subjects, which pales in comparison to the total number of professors in the UK: 30 among a total of 16,295 (Advance HE, 2018: 41; Black Female Professors Forum, n.d.; Rollock, 2019).

The problems of poor retention and the diminished likelihood of success are clearly significant, so my question was, and still is, what contribution can

I make to breaking down the barrier of White-dominated science? I identified two roles that are rooted in my science identity, as tools for acts of resistance that will bring change.

Breaking down barriers through acts of resistance: My role as a science educator

I have spent over twenty years working with students from ethnically and culturally diverse backgrounds and, before my science identity transformed me, I found the teaching challenging because I willingly bound myself to what was dictated to me about the style and content of my teaching. Why? Because my educational experience was devoid of any attempt to teach beyond what the establishment deemed to be important, and I followed suit and adhered strictly to a syllabus and style of teaching and assessment that were embedded in what convention dictated. I cannot pinpoint the moment when my approach to teaching changed; it was probably a gradual change building up against all the negative experiences that transformed my science identity. My concomitant redefinition of whose recognition mattered to me was liberating and joyful and gave rise to acts of resistance as I threw off the shackles of White, Eurocentric, patriarchal expectations that were thought appropriate in teaching science.

By teaching through the lens of a Black woman, I began to recognize that my role when I teach is not to dictate, be prescriptive, dominate or oppress my students so as to render them passive and powerless. My pedagogical approach is an act of resistance I have been developing since reading *Pedagogy of the Oppressed* by Paulo Freire (1970), recommended to me by a fellow member of the Ivory Tower/Black Sister Network. Although published almost fifty years ago, Freire's approach to students taking ownership of their learning through discussion and critical thinking is enlightening and sits perfectly with my altruistic science identity. I now see my role as a science educator who supports students in developing the confidence to be free to learn in their own way (although I am on hand to provide guidance and direction through dialogue). I am keen for my students to become innovative scientists who ask informed questions and challenge the norms set in the science academy for developing and delivering the curriculum they have been set to study.

What I teach is inextricably linked to how I teach. I feel compelled to acquire and share knowledge that questions science's objectivity in relation to race and gender, and to highlight how, due to racism, science has been the source of social injustice. I also want to increase awareness of the contribution of men and women of colour to science. Therefore, I see what I teach as an act of resistance driven by my altruistic identity and I now teach from a perspective that is increasingly culturally diverse. This approach is evident in my teaching of research ethics and nutrition but it was not always this way. In my early days as a lecturer, when I still adhered to White, Eurocentric, dominant norms, I limited my teaching of ethics to theoretical examples and used Eurocentric examples when teaching nutrition. I struggled to engage with the material.

It was during the transition from my disrupted identity to my altruistic science identity that I sought alternatives when I began rejecting the approval of the science academy that is entrenched in Whiteness. In research ethics I now use examples from the past and present that focus on those who were and are stigmatized because of their race, gender and class. I list some of them here: The Tuskegee syphilis trial (1934–72) (Centres for Disease Control and Prevention, 2019) was a study in which all the subjects (African-American men) were denied access to effective treatment for syphilis. I use this case as a classic example of human subjects being subordinated to scientific research. Also the HIV/AIDs prophylaxis studies in sub-Saharan Africa carried out in the 1990s, which were deemed to be unethical as they involved using placebos as controls despite the fact that a known effective prophylaxis was available (Angell, 1997: 847; Lurie and Wolfe, 1997: 853); and the work of marginalized groups to combat ethics dumping (Schroeder, 2018; Voice of the People, 2019). Ethics dumping is defined as failing to seek local ethics approval, undertaking research without the knowledge or consent of community leaders, or making public sensitive or personal information about indigenous groups.

In nutrition, I am aware that too often it is Eurocentric views, opinions and expertise that dominate problematic areas that impact on developing countries. One current and controversial issue is the development and use of genetically modified (GM) foods to address food insecurity. The voice of Western countries on this topic is loud so I seek out, teach and facilitate debate based on the knowledge and expertise of researchers from Africa, Asia, Europe and the Americas, as well as the experiences and views of communities themselves, whose lives have the potential to be affected, positively or negatively, by GM technology.

My role as a science educator with roots in an altruistic science identity has allowed me to thrive, but not in ways recognized by the science academy. My teaching has created an urgent demand for yet more knowledge in my sphere of expertise that is based on and produced by scientists from under-represented groups. I believe that science education seen through the lens of race and gender can give rise to questions that challenge the status quo. I hope this challenge will compel Black female (and male) students to pursue careers in science and drive research in areas that are focused on those who are under-represented, marginalized and stigmatized because of their race and gender.

I have no data, module evaluations, pass rates, progression data or testimonials from grateful students to present here as 'evidence' that my objectives for social justice education are being achieved. My intention when I embarked on this journey was largely focused on my own survival. However, the fact that my students actively and enthusiastically engage with my efforts, although at times they show trepidation at the newness of the material, helps affirm my approach and offers hope for the future. I end this part of my chapter with a quote that sums up why my role as a science educator can be used to break down barriers to STEM:

> The intersectional lens pushes us to ask new questions about the conditions under which talent can thrive. It expands and deepens our scientific understanding of lived experience and our predictive models in arenas as far-ranging as health and nutrition, environmental sustainability, and the nuances of the digital and cultural divides of our world. (Mack *et al.*, 2014)

Breaking down barriers through acts of resistance: My role as a mentor

In IT1 I wrote that 'mentoring is often critiqued as premised on a deficit model… (Gabriel, 2016)' and that 'it is used as a "single target" approach (Armstrong and Jovanovic, 2015: 145) to address the under-representation of Black women in STEM' (Opara, 2017: 130). I went on to explain how mentoring, and specifically being a mentee (in 2010–11), had benefited me, even though I was not professionally inadequate. My institution runs a number of mentoring schemes, and following my experience as a mentee I applied and trained to be a mentor, initially for the women-only scheme, which I enjoyed, but on reading the work of Settles *et al.* (2007: 270) I knew I had to change my focus. Let me elaborate: Settles *et al.* studied the impact of mentoring on women scientists' sense of voice in sexist environments. They found that woman-to-woman mentoring generated greater voice, which buffered the women from the damaging effects of sexism.

However, they did not examine how the race of the mentor or mentee might influence voice. Although I benefited from being mentored by a White woman, it became clear to me that the common lived experience of being a Black woman who is a scientist would be of even greater benefit to Black women scientists who seek a mentor. Black women in STEM are under-represented so are disadvantaged by being denied access to the informal yet effective and powerful networks accessible to their White colleagues. I began to understand how the role of mentor through the lens of intersectionality – my race and gender – could be used as an act of resistance to break down the barrier that is science. I applied and received training to be a mentor on my institution's Black and minority ethnic mentoring scheme and began to mentor Black women who were scientists or worked in healthcare in 2015. In the past year I have used my mentoring experience to support and guide Black women scientists outside the scheme or my institution who have sought my counsel as a result of my contribution to *Inside the Ivory Tower* (Gabriel and Tate, 2017) and my membership of the Black Sister Network. Those I have mentored spoke to me candidly, and at times emotionally, to express their frustrations at White colleagues who continually blocked their progress and refused to engage constructively. Examples of their experiences include:

- The Black woman scientist who questioned her place in science because she faced barriers in relation to being able to progress her research and was left on her own to deal with accusations of aggression, made by a White woman.
- The Black woman scientist who was overloaded with teaching and thus prevented from pursuing her research, whereas a White female colleague had her research time protected.
- The Black woman scientist who, despite constant praise by establishment figures for her creativity and motivation, was blocked from taking a leadership role.

Within these Black woman-on-Black woman mentoring experiences came opportunities for what Patricia Hill Collins calls self-definition and self-valuation, primarily because the mentoring experiences provided safe spaces that gave voice to both mentor and mentee (Hill Collins, 1986: 16; 2009: 111). We talked freely about the micro-aggressions perpetrated by White colleagues that stemmed from the stereotypical images of Black womanhood created, controlled and reinforced by their institutions and wider society. These spaces also empowered the challenging of these negative images, many of them 'distorted renderings' of the aspects of Black female behaviour seen as most threatening to 'White patriarchy' (Hill Collins, 1986: 17). A prime example of the 'distorted rendering' of our behaviour is the misrepresentation of the assertive, articulate, outspoken and strong Black woman. Such attributes are deemed unfeminine and thus the Black woman becomes the aggressor and the intimidator. These Black woman-on-Black woman mentoring spaces facilitated the rejection of such images and their replacement with 'authentic

Black female images' (ibid.) – images and attributes valued by us because they are us.

Hill Collins also talks about the different ways in which Black women experience and respond to the regular challenges of gender and racial discrimination (Hill Collins, 2009: 29) and the influence of social class. For example, she refers to literature which reports that the experiences of middle-class Black people are likely to be more pernicious and to leave them 'angry and disappointed' (Hill Collins, 2009: 31; Cose, 1993; Feagin and Sikes, 1994). Her analysis relates to my Black woman-mentor–Black women-mentee experience: the common challenge for middle-class Black women navigating a 'hostile environment' – i.e. the science academy – as representatives of an under-represented and stigmatized group. Their experiences were pernicious but seldom explicit, and equally hurtful were their responses of anger, disappointment, frustration and isolation. These Black women sought a safe space to talk to another middle-class Black woman (me) who had encountered a similar racism in the science academy and had responded in the same way. In our conversations, I drew on my own experiences and let them know that they did indeed matter and had a right to belong to the academy. I praised their achievements, and shared with them my own strategies for them to take back control and challenge those who tried to frustrate and block their progress.

This Black woman-to-Black woman relationship was invaluable as it allowed us to 'affirm one another's humanity, specialness and right to exist' (Hill Collins, 2009: 113). However, my analysis of this relationship, particularly in the context of social class, raises for me the question of how I would mentor a young Black woman from a working-class background who wishes to pursue a career in STEM, as her experiences of gender and racial discrimination are likely to be much more blatant (Hill Collins, 2009: 31). It is an impossible question for me to answer at present, but what I can say is that the commonality of our challenges, discipline and environment is a place to start.

The mentoring I have described and examined has given these women tools to protect themselves and to challenge attempts to undermine and isolate them. In addition, I too have benefited through the mentoring as I have maintained relationships with my mentees, some of whom are now mentors themselves. I have also increased my network of Black women scientists and am now part of the networks of the Black women I have mentored. It is clear, therefore, that Black woman-to-Black woman mentoring promotes the building of networks. Mack *et al.* (2014) argue that using an intersectional lens can drive 'us to seriously and systematically mentor the next generation of scientists in ways that empower…' and I believe this to be the case also for Black women scientists, be they early or established in their careers.

The mentoring of these women has been a privilege and I continue to thrive by helping them to find their voice and strengthing my own. There is clearly a personal and professional richness gained by me and those I have mentored that cannot be measured by performance metrics. However, I believe that this act of resistance can have a wider impact. Most of the mentoring I do is facilitated by my institution or, more specifically, elements within it, in the form of its Black and minority ethnic scheme, and this fact cannot be ignored. Through this mentoring scheme my institution could be an instrument for change. Jovanovic and Armstrong (2014: 4–5) recognize this possibility but they assert that academic institutions must support and engage with the networks of Black women in STEM who are empowered to define their own needs, learn, support, guide, nurture, instruct, inform, grow, survive and thrive. This level of engagement needs to be sincere and forthright to generate profound and transformational change at the institutional level, so that academia can become an inclusive, and thus complete, centre of learning and innovation in STEM (ibid.).

Academic institutions should also consider including other members of the science academy in allying with Black women in STEM and their networks. A recent study by Johnson *et al.* (2019: 131) reported that in addition to Black women role models providing a sense of belonging to young Black women STEM students, these same students discerned allies among White women role models. It is possible therefore that in conjunction with Black woman-to-Black woman mentoring and working with networks of Black women in the science academy, White women science academics have a contribution to make in the fight against the status quo of White male dominance of the science academy. However, and chiming with Jovanovic and Armstrong (2014: 4–5), Johnson *et al.* (2019: 131) recognize that for White women to make a sustained contribution they must be trustworthy, accepting the standpoint and 'unique challenges' faced by young Black women students in the science academy and demonstrating an earnest commitment to helping Black women thrive in their chosen STEM subject by working alongside them to break down the gender and racial discrimination that impede their success.

Transformation at institutional level could be a long way off when there are relatively few Black women in STEM in academia. This limits the availability of Black women to mentor others and the growth of their networks. However, the numbers are there at undergraduate level so strategies and acts of resistance that compel or inspire students to stay and pursue careers in

STEM, particularly in academia, such as my role as a science educator, are essential.

Conclusion

My chapter is about how my altruistic science identity has compelled me to adopt strategies and acts of resistance to break down the barrier that is science, its teaching, practice and institutions at local level. It is also a personal journey and account of how I thrive in the science academy by using this identity. I hope that it will inspire Black women scientists in academia, especially those who are embarking on their careers and those who, like me, have struggled or are struggling with isolation, borne of a lack of voice. My altruistic science identity is manifested through my work as a science educator and mentor but it is not constrained to these roles. Other roles are possible through which resistance leads to change. The role of researcher comes to mind because of the under-representation of scientists of colour, the lack of recognition for the importance of their research and the high value of inclusive scientific research. I chose the roles of science educator and mentor because these are the roles in which my altruistic identity has had the most profound effect, and also the roles in which I believe I can have the greatest impact on the barriers to STEM. The power of these roles is, I believe, borne out by studies that support the efficacy of exposing young Black women to successful role models to inoculate them against misrepresentative and belittling stereotypes that might persuade them that they have no place in the science academy (Pietri *et al.*, 2018: 192; Johnson *et al.*, 2019: 131).

In my role as science educator I strive to increase my cultural competences and those of my students by expanding their learning to the experience, knowledge and expertise of scientists from marginalized and under-represented groups who work in the areas I teach. My efforts to decolonize the science curriculum come when the imbalance in the teaching of science in universities is being challenged (Kruger, 2018; Nordling, 2018; Roy, 2018). The current emphasis of the science curriculum is primarily on past and present glories and pursuits of scientific knowledge that are Eurocentric and/or perceived to be dependent on the expertise and financial aid of Western countries and former colonizers. This emphasis portrays Black people and their contributions to science as non-existent, inferior or insignificant (Nordling, 2018; Roy, 2018). In my role as a science educator I am seeking to make it clear that no single group has 'cultural superiority' (Roy, 2018). Black scientists are leading research in areas that yield insights necessary for the advancement of their communities, countries and continents

(Guglielmi, 2018; Kruger, 2018; Nordling, 2018; Roy, 2018). However, I need to do more to expand the curriculum I teach. I am unsure whether I can achieve this but I have begun to explore the matter.

As a mentor, my ultimate aim is achieving solidarity through sisterhood: a strong, robust and resilient sisterhood that is not influenced by the hegemonic dominance of White males and their slow-to-change attitudes to gender and race. Reflection on my analysis of the Black woman mentor–mentee relationship convinces me that this sisterhood must be built on our commonality and learning from and about our diversity and uniqueness (Hill Collins, 2009: 107; hooks, 1984: 43).

bell hooks (1984: 58) put it like this: 'When women of colour strive to learn with and about one another we take responsibility for building sisterhood.' And, she writes, 'To experience solidarity, we must have a community of interests, shared beliefs, and goals to unite, to build Sisterhood.' (hooks: 1984: 64).

I will continue to work to help build a strong and cohesive network of Black women scientists in academia that can organize and transform its members at local level and will aim to extend this approach, through mentoring, to other Black women scientists, including, potentially, the next generation of scientists who are unsure about pursuing a career in the science academy. Empowerment through mentoring can be achieved in academic institutions that have appropriate mentoring schemes – ideally one for Black women science academics, or otherwise a scheme that provides opportunities for intersectional mentoring, for example a women or Black minority ethnic scheme.

On the surface, the approaches I discuss may appear simple but it has taken me a long time to reach this point and I have a long way to go before I can say with confidence that my method of tackling barriers to STEM has had an impact at institutional level, which is my goal. Some may say this is a lofty ambition but I believe it is possible because it is only through the lens of race and gender that Black women in the science academy can resist, thrive and ultimately drive its transformation.

References

Anonymous Academic (2019) 'Nobody takes responsibility for tackling racism in my university. Why?' Online. www.theguardian.com/education/2019/mar/29/nobody-takes-responsibility-for-tackling-racism-in-my-university-why (accessed 12 January 2020).

AdvancedHE (2018) *Equality + higher education: staff statistical report*. Online. www.advance-he.ac.uk/resources/2018_HE-stats-report-staff.pdf (accessed 09/05/19).

Angell, M. (1997) 'The ethics of clinical research in the Third World'. *New England Journal of Medicine*, 337 (12), 847–9.

Armstrong, M.A. and Jovanovic, J. (2015) 'Starting at the crossroads: Intersectional approaches to institutionally supporting underrepresented minority women STEM faculty'. *Journal of Women and Minorities in Science and Engineering*, 21 (2), 141–57.

Bhopal, K. (2018) 'White privilege'. In Bhopal, K. *White Privilege: The myth of a post-racial society.* Bristol: Policy Press.

Black Female Professors Forum (n.d) Online. https://blackfemaleprofessorsforum. org/ (accessed 12 January 2020).

British Science Association (n.d) *Diversity and Inclusion.* Online. www. britishscienceassociation.org/diversity-and-inclusion (accessed 08/05/19).

Carlone, H.B. and Johnson, A. (2007) 'Understanding the science experiences of successful women of color: Science identity as an analytic lens'. *Journal of Research in Science Teaching*, 44 (8), 1187–1218.

CaSE (Campaign for Science and Engineering) (2014) 'Improving Diversity in STEM: A report by the Campaign for Science and Engineering (CaSE)'. Online. http://sciencecampaign.org.uk/CaSEDiversityinSTEMreport2014.pdf (accessed 12 January 2020).

Centres for Disease Control and Prevention (2019) 'The Tuskegee Timeline'. Online. www.cdc.gov/tuskegee/timeline.htm (accessed 12 January 2020).

Cose, E. (1993) *The Rage of a Privileged Class.* New York: HaperCollins.

Curtis, D. (2018) 'Polygenic risk score for schizophrenia is more strongly associated with ancestry than with schizophrenia'. *Psychiatric Genetics*, 28 (5), 85–9.

Devlin, H. (2018) 'Genetics research "biased towards studying white Europeans"'. Online. www.theguardian.com/science/2018/oct/08/genetics-research-biased-towards-studying-white-europeans (accessed 12 January 2020).

Durkin, E. (2019) 'DNA scientist James Watson stripped of honors over views on race'. Online. www.theguardian.com/world/2019/jan/13/james-watson-scientist-honors-stripped-reprehensible-race-comments (accessed 12 January 2020).

Feagin, J.R. and Sikes, M.P. (1994) *Living with Racism: The black middle class experience.* Boston: Beacon.

Freire, P. (1970) *Pedagogy of the Oppressed.* London: Penguin.

Gabriel, D. (2016) *Will Lack of Career Progression Drive Black Female Academics Overseas?* Online. http://blacksisternetwork.blackbritishacademics. co.uk/2016/11/18/will-lack-of-career-progression-drive-black-female-academics-overseas/ (accessed 8 March 2017).

Gabriel, D. (2018) 'Social closure, White male privilege and female complicity: Why gender equality still has a long way to go'. Online. https://deborahgabriel. com/2018/10/28/social-closure-white-male-privilege-and-female-complicity-why-gender-equality-still-has-a-long-way-to-go/ (accessed 12 January 2020).

Gabriel, D. and Tate, S.A. (eds) (2017) *Inside the Ivory Tower: Narratives of women of colour surviving and thriving in British academia.* London: Trentham Books.

Guglielmi, G. (2019) 'Facing up to genome injustice'. *Nature*, 568, 290–3.

Hill Collins, P. (1986) 'Learning from the outsider within: The sociological significance of Black feminist thought'. *Social Problems*, 33 (6), S14–S32.

Hill Collins, P. (2009) 'The power of self-definition'. *In Black Feminist Thought:*

Knowledge, consciousness, and the politics of empowerment. 2nd ed. London: Routledge, 107–32.

hooks, b. (1984) 'Sisterhood: Political solidarity between women'. In *Feminist Theory from Margin to Center.* Boston: South End Press.

Jefferson, E. (2019) 'Where are the Black women in STEM leadership?' Online. https://blogs.scientificamerican.com/voices/where-are-the-black-women-in-stem-leadership/ (accessed 12 January 2020).

Johnson, I., Pietri, E.S., Fullilove, F. and Mowrer, S. (2019) 'Exploring identity-safety cues and allyship among Black women students in STEM environments'. *Psychology of Women Quarterly*, 43 (2), 131–50.

Jovanovic, J. and Armstrong, M.A. (2014) 'Mission possible: Empowering institutions with strategies for change'. *peerReview*, 16 (2). Online. www.aacu.org/publications-research/periodicals/mission-possible-empowering-institutions-strategies-change (accessed 12 January 2020).

Kruger, N. (2018) 'Science deans forum: Decolonising science, determining knowledge and developing graduates'. Online. www.uwc.ac.za/Faculties/NS/News/Pages/Science-Deans-Forum-Decolonising-Science,-Determining-Knowledge-and-Developing-Graduates.aspx (accessed 12 January 2020).

Lurie, P. and Wolfe, S.M. (1997) 'Unethical trials of intervention to reduce perinatal transmission of the human immunodeficiency virus in developing countries'. *New England Journal of Medicine*, 337 (12), 853–6.

Mack, K., Orlando, T., Cantor, N. and McDermott, P. (2014) 'If not now, when? The promise of STEM intersectionality in the twenty-first century'. *peerReview*, 16 (2). Online. www.aacu.org/publications-research/periodicals/if-not-now-when-promise-stem-intersectionality-twenty-first (accessed 12 January 2020).

Nordling, L. (2018) 'South African science faces its future'. *Nature*, 554, 159–62.

Opara, E. (2017) 'The transformation of my science identity'. In Gabriel, D. and Tate, S.A. (eds), *Inside the Ivory Tower: Narratives of women of colour surviving and thriving in British academia.* London: Trentham Books, 124–35.

Pietri, E.S., Johnson, I.R. and Ozgumus, E. (2018) 'One size may not fit all: Exploring how the intersection of race and gender and stigma consciousness predict effective identity-safe cues for Black women'. *Journal of Experimental Social Psychology*, 74, 291–306.

Rollock, N. (2019) 'Staying Power: The career experiences and strategies of UK Black female professors'. Online. www.ucu.org.uk/media/10075/staying-power/pdf/ucu_rollock_february_2019.pdf (accessed 12 January 2020).

Roy, R.D. (2018) 'Decolonize science: Time to end another imperial era'. Online. https://theconversation.com/decolonize-science-time-to-end-another-imperial-era-89189 (accessed 12 January 2020).

Rutherford, A. (2014) 'He may have unravelled DNA, but James Watson deserves to be shunned'. Online. www.theguardian.com/commentisfree/2014/dec/01/dna-james-watson-scientist-selling-nobel-prize-medal (accessed 12 January 2020).

Sayed, M. (2016) 'How objective is science, really?' Online. https://thetempest.co/2016/09/16/now-beyond/science/how-objective-is-science/ (accessed 12 January 2020).

Schroeder, D. (2018) 'Ethics dumping: The exploitative side of academic research'. Online. www.theguardian.com/higher-education-network/2018/aug/31/ethics-dumping-the-exploitative-side-of-academic-research (accessed 12 January 2020).

Settles, I.H., Cortina, L.M., Stewart, A.J. and Malley, J. (2007) 'Voice Matters: Buffering the impact of a negative climate for women in science'. *Psychology of Women Quarterly*, 31, 270–81.

Voice of the People (2019) 'UCT adopts global research ethics code'. Online. www.radiovop.com/uct-adopts-global-research-ethics-code/# (accessed 25/04/19).

Weikart, R. (2018) 'Is science objective? Steven Pinker's counterattack against the "War on Science"'. Online. https://evolutionnews.org/author/rweikart/page/2/ (accessed 12 January 2020).

WISE: A campaign to promote women in science, technology and engineering (2014) '"Not for people like me?" Under-represented groups in science, technology and engineering – a summary of the evidence: the facts, the fiction and what we should do next'. Online. www.wisecampaign.org.uk/wp-content/uploads/2018/06/not_for_people_like_me-full-report.pdf (accessed 12 January 2020).

Chapter 4

Emancipatory research on FGM policy with women of African descent
Ima Jackson

Introduction

This chapter analyses the theoretical basis, strategic approach and practical implications of developing research centred on engaging with communities of colour and migrants in Scotland to inform policy, research, education and service planning. It examines a project I led, called Enhancing Transcultural Participation in Policy and Practice Through Preventing FGM. I designed it primarily to give voice and empowerment to women of African descent who felt marginalized in the process of national consultation relating to female genital mutilation (FGM) in Scotland. I led on the development of research with community organizers, individual participants and researchers who were women and girls of African descent wanting to explore the policy, practice and service provision to support learning about FGM policy. It aimed to be rooted in the knowledge and experience of the affected women and to support communities taking effective action to prevent FGM. I also sought to develop a methodology for this kind of research that could also be applied in other settings. This research enhances race and gender equality by prioritizing and giving voice to the knowledge and expertise within communities about an experience that directly affects them, and subverting policy and research that has marginalized and excluded them. An academic for over fifteen years, I have worked with communities of colour, the new and the long-established migrants in Scotland. In *Inside the Ivory Tower* (published by Trentham Boks in 2017, for convenience IT1), I analysed my stance and experiences of direct sustained engagement with communities of colour in Scotland and how this helped to give me a much-needed sense of belonging. I created an opportunity to understand how the system excludes through ongoing intellectual interrogation of people of colour during events, in discussions or while I supported the development of community-led projects. I did this to truly understand the system of exclusion from their marginalized perspective and to escape the hegemony of academia. I sought to identify supportive spaces within organizations where people of colour might safely and authoritatively communicate their own knowledge, experiences and expertise. I have long been aware of whose narrative is viewed as universal in Scotland, whose experience is valued and seen as expert. I combined my knowledge of the traditional system of creating evidence for policy and practice and the experience of communities of colour to at times disrupt processes in ways that I believe are supportive to the ambitions of all.

Working directly with communities in academia helps me maintain my perspective that community expertise and expert knowledge need to influence the decisions dominating their lives. Although slowly changing, it remains rare to find academics of colour working in Scotland. It is even rarer in Scotland to find colleagues like me working explicitly with those who are racialized.

This chapter focuses on one example of such work centred on FGM. Below I first set out the significance of Scotland's erasure of its deep involvement in the transatlantic slave trade and suggest how that can become articulated in the current context of its policy and research. Next, I outline the theoretical framing and influences developing my approach to understanding this landscape. Last, I describe some of the strategies I use to develop transformational work that enhances race and gender equality.

Historical amnesia and the peculiarity of the Scottish context

The socio-geographical and historical context of Scotland is important to this study. Scotland has experienced significant levels of unprecedented immigration over the past twenty years. Its demographic has fundamentally changed, and that transition continues to develop. The proportion of people of colour living in Scotland has doubled in each census from 1990, reaching 12 per cent in 2011. Twenty-one per cent of children at primary school in 2014 had a non-white background and Glasgow's overall non-white population is expected to reach 19 per cent by 2031 (Walsh *et al.*, 2018). Universities, policy and practice are struggling to adapt to this changing demographic profile. Scotland is comfortable with its immigrant history as it appears unrelated to its role in the transatlantic slave trade:

> The Scots are one of the world's greatest nations of emigrants. For centuries, untold numbers of men, women and children have sought their fortunes in every conceivable walk of life and in every imaginable climate. All over the British Empire, the United States

and elsewhere, the Scottish contribution to the development of the modern world has been a formidable one ... (Devine, 2011: 8)

Devine is arguably Scotland's most populist historian, who had contributed to the generational erasure of Scotland's involvement in the transatlantic slave trade. However, in 2015 he began to rethink his work:

For more than a century and a half the real story of Scotland's connections to transatlantic slavery has been lost to history and shrouded in myth. There was even denial that the Scots, unlike the English, had any significant involvement in slavery. Scotland saw itself as a pioneering abolitionist nation untainted by a slavery past. (Devine, 2015: 4)

I focus on this aspect of history because the hegemony, dominant cultural narrative and this erasure impact the day-to-day experience of people of colour in Scotland. There may have been few enslaved people living in Scotland, but its wealth originated from the practice of slavery and the country is only now beginning to publicly accept this. In the words of Trinidadian Eric Williams: 'Slavery was not born of racism: rather, racism was the consequence of slavery.' Scotland's role in the transatlantic slave trade and the impact on people of colour is rarely explored but it is borne out by the persistent racism documented in reports spanning years of inequality and discrimination (Coalition for Racial Equality and Rights, 2011; Strang, Baillot and Mignard, 2016; Lyle, 2017; Scottish Government, 2017; Jackson, 2018). Scotland's colonial past, involvement in the transatlantic slave trade, the racialization of people to sustain that trade and its subsequent erasure of that history also impact the experience of recent migrants. My work with migrant communities is in part sustained through personally witnessing over the past twenty years that relatively new migrants from the African Diaspora experience racial micro- and macro-aggressions and discrimination in their daily lives.

FGM and the new interest in FGM in Scotland

FGM is practised within some African communities. It has become increasingly evident that excluding African communities from making decisions – on education about FGM – has diverted attention from the violence it subjects women and girls to and may even have aided the illegal practice. FGM has no health benefits and harms girls and women in many ways, removing and damaging healthy genital tissue and interfering with their bodies' natural functions (Wasige and Jackson, 2018).

In Scotland a policy participation strategy encourages interaction between different communities and cultures. It had been anticipated that the Community Empowerment (Scotland) Act 2015 (Scottish Government, 2015) might help to support this relatively new phenomenon to Scotland. FGM commands the attention of health services, child protection, police, the prosecutor general and educational services. The Scottish Government acknowledges that not only is a multi-sectoral approach required to deal with FGM but that affected communities must lead on naming the problem and designing the solutions (Scottish Government, 2016).

However, despite consultation on strengthening protections for FGM in October 2018, the consultation and community work surrounding it did not feel safe and responsive to the women who were participating. With a view to developing a proposed agenda of FGM, I learned from the community organizers working to support the consultation that some of the women felt that their viewpoints were not taken into consideration and therefore their contribution to the consultation was limited. Some said they felt co-opted and criminalized by the processes as communities have felt previously when they have only an option to speak and must engage within the parameters already set (Hill Collins, 1990). I became as disappointed and frustrated as the FGM community campaigners and activists. Together we discussed the process of consultation, policy participation and whether the intimacy of the issue could help me understand how the system co-opts them. Along with a community worker from the Kenyan Women in Scotland Association (KWISA), we developed a research proposal to explore issues of engagement. We planned to examine the processes of consultation, policy engagement and research on FGM in Scotland, and articulate and evidence the knowledge, expertise and solutions the community held.

The research project was therefore developed by women of African descent, engaging with me as a local Black female academic. Through informal conversations I came to understand how, despite sustained efforts at consultation in Scotland, some women felt marginalized by a process that was ostensibly for them as their input was not embedded as hoped. Together we decided to research how their voices could be respected and centred. They trusted me to develop an approach with them. Together we explored how their experience of voicelessness, marginalization and co-option is documented and understood by Black feminist scholars such as Patricia Hill Collins (1990). We used a fusion of Black feminist thought and critical race theory (CRT) to examine both the Black women's experience and the theoretical clarifications about how the issue had become racialized and marginalized:

Investigating the subjugated knowledge of subordinate groups – in this case a Black women's standpoint and Black feminist thought – requires more ingenuity than that needed to examine the standpoints and thought of dominant groups. I found my training as a social scientist inadequate to the task of studying the subjugated knowledge of a Black woman's standpoint. This is because subordinate groups have long had to use alternative ways to create independent self-definitions and self-valuations and to rearticulate them through our own specialists. Like other subordinate groups, African American women have not only developed a distinctive Black women's standpoint, but have done so by using alternative ways of producing and validating knowledge. (Hill Collins, 2000: 252)

This small study was developed with African communities in Scotland who felt dissonance and disconnect between what they were saying and what was being heard within a national consultation process. Our overall ambition was to co-create research with women and girls from communities that potentially practised FGM, support their ambition to be given time and space to think about the issues that affect them, and direct that into policy and practice. We aimed to feed the findings from the direct experiences of working with those affected and to explore the system of knowledge exchange within policy and education concerning FGM. Specific details of the research results are not reported here, as it is the contextualizing of the research itself into strategies to transform community research that I focus on here. There was a deep disconnect between what the women wished to enact in the communities and what was determined within the national consultation process as being of value. The marginalization of African women in policy and practice was manifesting in ways that neither the communities involved, nor the policy-makers and service planners, had anticipated or could easily understand.

As I came to understand the implications of academic isolation as explored in my chapter in IT1, I sought greater understanding of the landscape through Black feminist literature. This helped me reframe my engagement with communities I relied on for support and belonging. I began to view myself as an academic activist. In her essay *The Master's Tools Will Never Dismantle the Master's House,* Audre Lorde explores the exclusion and isolation of Black women's perspectives in the feminist movement:

Advocating the mere tolerance of difference between women is the grossest reformism. It is a total denial of the creative function of difference in our lives. Difference must not merely be tolerated but seen as a fund of necessary polarities. Difference is that raw and powerful connection from which our personal power is forged.... Without community there is no liberation but community must not mean a shedding of our differences, nor the pathetic pretence that these differences do not exist. (Lorde, 2017: 18)

More than thirty years later I still find Lorde's words inspiring and instructive. They question who has the knowledge and expertise to understand our experiences as Black women and thus support our collaboration in this small study in Scotland. The women who engaged with me in the research were determined to bring their knowledge to the fore because in the past their perspectives were merely tolerated rather than viewed as expert knowledge. The framing of migrants and other racialized groups has become more polarized and contentious in recent years. I therefore view an important part of my academic role as identifying, making visible and, where possible, reducing systemic obstacles to communication to facilitate collaborative working.

Developing strategies to transform public policy research

In IT1 I reflected on how I framed my experience in academia as a Scottish experience, rather than as a Black female scholar. The strength and support I gained from realizing quite late in my career how typical my experience has been encouraged me to develop my approach to transformative practice. Sara Ahmed's (2012) work helped develop my thinking towards a practical and direct understanding of negotiating strategies. Her exploration of the role and function of diversity work in higher education deepened my understanding of organizational dynamics around race in knowledge production, and I applied it to the articulation of Black women's experience around public policy research on FGM. Below are seven strategies I developed and adopted for my emancipatory research on FGM policy.

1: Grounding the research with the women

Hill Collins' ('Learning from the outsider within: The sociological significance of Black feminist thought' (1986) has been a major influence on my navigation of my role in academia as an 'outsider-within' and my approach to emancipatory research with Black women. As Hill Collins said in a later work:

Oppressed groups are frequently placed in the situation of being listened to only if we frame our ideas in the language that is familiar to and comfortable for the dominant group. This requirement often changes the meaning of our ideas and works to elevate the ideas of the dominant group. (Hill Collins, 1990: vii)

I grounded my research with the women whose intimate experiences needed to be included in the policy and practice. My solution to academic isolation was to seek direct engagement with communities of colour. Determining that the sites for knowledge production lay with the women came out of my reality as an isolated researcher in Scotland and I found our mutual support and trust sustained our growing shared knowledge.

2: *Paying attention to the history of commodification of FGM*

Postcolonial and African feminist critiques of Western feminism have brought important perspectives to understanding how some cultures maintained FGM because they clarify how even those who seek to eradicate the practice have contributed to its continuation; they are able to reflect on their own stance and the cultural and historical perspectives in which they themselves are situated. In the 1990s, postcolonial theorists such as Abusharaf (2006), Nnaemeka and Ezeilo (2005), Gruenbaum (2001), Walley (1997) and Toubia (1994) argue that Western feminists frame FGM as a measure of cultural inferiority, therefore positioning African men and women as objects of intervention, not subjects in their own right (Wasige and Jackson, 2018). There have been incidents in Scotland that Wasige and Jackson (2018) describe as the sensitization of FGM by the public and the media's triggering of what hooks (1992) calls *eating the other*: the commodification of FGM as a playground in which dominating races affirm their power over intimate relationships with FGM communities. Portrayed as barbaric, cruel and victims of their own culture, White-led organizations win funding bids to 'save' women of African descent and so affirm their superiority.

3: *Valuing the intellectual capital of community participants*

The nature of funding contributes to neo-colonialism and inequality in research. If I problematize the experience of people of colour, I find that research funding is likely to be awarded but if I seek to explore the wider issues, funding is generally less forthcoming. This proscribed focus for research both reflects and manifests the power dynamics within our research funding structures as Hill Collins powerfully argues:

> Not just elite group support, but the endorsement of subordinated groups is needed for hegemonic ideologies to function smoothly. Realizing that Black feminist demands for social justice threaten existing power hierarchies, organizations must find ways of appearing to include African American women – reversing historical patterns of social exclusion associated with institutional discrimination – while disempowering us. (Hill Collins, 2000: 284)

As Zimunya (2019) explains, 'there are clear rewards if you respond within funding calls in the way that the funders determine is the way the issue is to be viewed'. My approach with our study was to seek out a Scottish Government and EU social innovation call where community participants are costed as experts on their own experiences so their costs mirror those of the researchers. They were paid not as participants but as equal partners, and this was an important foundation of our collaborative work.

4: Learning from each other – centring our perspectives.

Most importantly, learning from the women and girls how they manage their interpersonal relationships within a culture where FGM persists within their racialized lives in Scotland, we explored the lexicon they developed to discuss FGM or their racialized lives more generally. We looked at their experiences together, with peers, parents, wider family and friends as well as with potential academic allies, and the language they use to engage with professionals. This represented a co-creation of new knowledge, identified in Black feminist literature:

> For Black women, new knowledge claims are rarely worked out in isolation from other individuals and are usually developed through dialogues with other members of a community. A primary epistemological assumption underlying the use of dialogue in assessing knowledge claims is that connectedness rather than separation is an essential component of the knowledge validation process. (Belenky *et al.*, 1986, cited in Hill Collins, 2000: 260)

Black feminist standpoint theory helped me recognize that individual and collective expertise is the core knowledge required to develop an appropriate policy and practice response to Black women's needs concerning FGM. I regard my academic role as one which develops processes that enable community expertise to be valued and incorporated as evidence within the register of FGM policy, research and service planning in Scotland. I am uncomfortable writing this chapter as I was the project lead, but the women, girls, researchers and community organization were central to the research project. I cannot emphasize too strongly that this study was a collective and collaborative effort.

5: Ensuring safety and self-care

A key consideration for this study was ensuring an appropriate environment for learning and sharing that suited various groups such as the project steering team, the community staff team, the community participants and schoolgirls. I focused on ensuring that the participants understood the importance of how to manage each other's time and efforts respectfully, especially when talking about difficult matters. We developed protocols to support colleagues when people felt uncomfortable with what they were hearing or sharing, or were upset by participating. We recognized the importance of culturally relevant food such as jollof rice, chicken and fruit, in shaping the learning environment, and we organized the after-learning sessions. I kept Lorde's (1988: 130) words circulating in our work together: 'caring for myself is not self indulgence, it is an act of political warfare'. Self-care and kindness were openly talked about as healing and nurturing, which I needed in our shared research. Debriefing was offered among staff who were practised at managing sensitive issues.

6: Action learning sets as tools for transformative outputs

I used action learning sets as the base framework for the study. We explored a variety of concepts through presentations together with self-directed learning and peer support. This required us to think carefully and to listen to the women's experiences as each week of teaching, learning and exploration was developed. Drawing on Hill Collins (2009), Mirza (2006) and Ahmed (2004), I was mindful that the expertise held in the community was the knowledge I needed to develop appropriate educational material for staff, students and policy-makers to learn so as to ensure that the women and girls, the community, research staff and policy-makers all brought their varied expertise into the research environment. One aspect of the research involved some community participants interviewing policy-makers about their expertise and experiences. I adopted this approach so I could facilitate the flatter hierarchy of knowledge exchange that allowed me to use more innovative tools in research.

7: Recognizing the value of inter-generational learning

Anti-FGM work in Kenya has stressed the importance of inter-generational exchange in dealing with FGM. Their approach is to develop alternative initiation processes for those in Kenya whose FGM practice is a rite of passage rather than something carried out soon after birth. Setting out their learning approaches they argue:

> It may be advantageous to participants to create 'safe space' protocols for some aspects of this research. Alternatively, it may be possible to develop specific biocultural community protocols (BCPs) that safeguard participants from being adversely affected by their involvement in the research. It is advisable to engage with cultural/religious guides during research – highly respected community or religious leaders who are familiar with the cultural

and religious sensibilities/politics around FGM and child marriage.
(Oloo, Wanjiru and Newell-Jones, 2011: 30)

Our learning in Scotland became inter-generational when work undertaken by the older women was described with such skill that the younger generations were able to understand what was being shared and grow in confidence. In turn, the younger women's use of social media to share their experiences supported the older women who found publicly sharing information to be challenging.

Conclusion

I define myself as a community-engaged academic whose work sits within the broad context of transcultural practice and migration. By centring my work around people of colour and migrants I have developed a research approach that produces evidence that incorporates the perspectives of subjects who are racialized and marginalized. Leading the study entailed helping to maintain a flat hierarchy of expertise, which is paramount when the subjects of the research and policy are rarely involved in the decision-making process. I work specifically with communities of colour and migrants in Scotland, developing mechanisms with communities to support colleagues in academia, in policy and practice, to recognize and include the expertise held by the communities themselves about their own experiences. This work builds on the recognition that for people of colour in Scotland, the presentation of their experiences in education and research can become racialized (Coalition for Racial Equality and Rights, 2011; Mirza, 2015; Grange, 2016; Jackson, 2018; Wasige and Jackson, 2018).

This began when I became immersed in the mainstream approaches to research and knowledge development, supported by my background in nursing and midwifery. In my doctoral study I used discourse analysis to investigate the dynamics of interprofessional relationships within and surrounding midwifery practice, and I evidenced the power differentials and tensions experienced by midwives through acceptance of and resistance to the dominance of medical knowledge within their sphere of practice (Jackson, 2005). This, combined with CRT and Black feminism, formed the basis of my approach to articulating and evidencing the experiences of racialized communities to one other, to colleagues in academia, policy-makers and service planners so as to critically reflect on the processes and structures we are all engaged in.

Much of the work was focused on developing appropriate ways to engage with the knowledge of the community participants and then translate that expertise into practice. This was achieved by engaging in regular feedback sessions, where discussions were held regarding the different meanings of living within communities who might practise FGM and the way that FGM was taught, both to them and about them. They were supported in identifying and focusing on the differing perspectives, the language used and the general dissonance in which the community was seeking space to explore the issues whereas the policy and literature focused on criminalizing the activities of these communities.

The transformational potential of the work was clear to see at the dissemination launch. The project report launch was led by the young women, with Christina McKelvie (Minister for Older People and Equality) and Eva Bolander (Lord Provost of Glasgow). The young women's faces glowed with pride as they saw the importance of the work they had done expressed through the appreciation of the older women, senior colleagues and media interest. I believe that their sense of themselves, their sense of agency and of their own potential was fundamentally changed by that experience. The interweaving of experience, the inter-generational aspects of the work and the ways of knowing are encapsulated in Black feminist thought:

> While these ways of knowing are not gender specific, disproportionate numbers of women rely on connected knowing. Separate knowers try to subtract the personality of an individual from his or her ideas because they see personality as biasing those ideas. In contrast, connected knowers see personality as adding to an individual's ideas and feel that the personality of each group member enriches a group's understanding. The significance of individual uniqueness, personal expressiveness, and empathy in African American communities thus resembles the importance that some feminist analyses place on women's 'inner voice'. (Belenky *et al.*, 1986, cited in Hill Collins, 2000: 274)

My main objective for the study was to ensure that the knowledge and experience of Black women and girls from the African diasporic communities in Scotland was recognized as the expertise required to understand and feed into the policy and practice framework on FGM. The drive and the ability to develop and sustain this way of working came out of the experience of being an isolated academic. It came out of my recognition that relying on direct engagement with those who are racialized, to centre my work within their experiences, was of immense support to me personally. This approach is one that ensures women's knowledge can be formed and shared in ways that do not to become part of the framework that at times can weaponize communities' experiences against themselves, racialize their experiences, misunderstand or ignore them. By working in a co-creative partnership, the women were supported in sharing their way of knowing and their narratives of expertise in a way that counteracts dominant epistemologies:

> Black feminist thought fosters a fundamental paradigmatic shift in how we think about unjust power relations. By embracing a paradigm of intersecting oppressions of race, class, gender, sexuality and nation, as well as Black women's individual and collective agency within them, Black feminist thought reconceptualizes the social relations of domination and resistance. Second, Black feminist thought addresses ongoing epistemological debates concerning the power dynamics that underlie what counts as knowledge. (Hill Collins, 2000: 274)

My contribution to race and gender equality as highlighted in this chapter was to develop an approach to support a community of Black African women to recognize and value the knowledge and expertise they have drawn from experience that now challenges them and that they are keen to address. I hope this critical reflection is useful for researchers and communities who wish to explore a transformational approach to public policy research. Diverse experiences and knowledge are increasingly more likely to present themselves, not only because of the direct reality of Scotland's demographic changes, but also because of the growing understanding of Whiteness and the manifestations of White hegemony within our institutions.

References

Abusharaf, M.J. (ed.) (2006) *Female Circumcision: Multicultural perspectives*. Philadelphia: University of Pennsylvania Press.

Advance HE (2018) 'Equality + higher education: Staff statistical report 2018'. Online. https://tinyurl.com/ycjlamgs (accessed 12 January 2020).

Ahmed, S. (2004) 'Declarations of whiteness: The non-performativity of anti-racism'. *borderlands*, 30 (2), 1–15.

Ahmed, S. (2012) *On Being Included: Racism and diversity in institutional life*. Durham, NC: Duke University Press.

Coalition for Racial Equality and Rights (2011) *Scottish Identity and Black and Minority Ethnic Communities in Scotland: An introductory review of literature*. Glasgow: Coalition for Racial Equality and Rights. Available at: www.crer.org. uk/Publications/Identity.pdf (Accessed: 9 March 2017).

Devine, T.M. (2011) *Scotland's Empire: The origins of the global diaspora*. London: Penguin.

Devine, T.M. (ed.) (2015) *Recovering Scotland's Slavery Past: The Caribbean connection*. Edinburgh: Edinburgh University Press.

Gabriel, D. and Tate, S.A. (eds) (2017) *Inside the Ivory Tower: Narratives of women of colour surviving and thriving in British academia*. London: Trentham Books.

Grange, L.L. (2016) 'Decolonising the university curriculum'. *South African Journal of Higher Education*, 30 (2), 259. Online. doi: 10.20853/30-2-709 (accessed 12 January 2020).

Gruenbaum, E. (2001) *The Female Circumcision Controversy: An anthropological perspective*. Philadelphia: University of Pennsylvania Press.

Hill Collins, P. (1986) 'Learning from the outsider within: The sociological significance of Black feminist thought'. *Social Problems*, 33 (6), 14–32.

Hill Collins, P. (1990) *Black Feminist Thought: Knowledge, consciousness and the politics of empowerment*. New York: Unwin Hyman; 2nd ed. London: Routledge, 2000.

Hill Collins, P. (2009) *Another Kind of Public Education: Race, schools, the media, and democratic possibilities*. Boston: Beacon Press.

hooks, b. (1992) *Black Looks: Race and representation*. Boston: South End Press.

Jackson, I. (2005) *'Midwives Talk': A discourse analysis of midwives' experience of hospital based maternity care in a Scottish city*. Glasgow Caledonian University.

Jackson, I. (2018) 'Immigration to Scotland from overseas: The experience of nurses'. In Devine, T.M. and McCarthy, A. (eds) *New Scots: Scotland's immigrant communities since 1945*, 273.

Lorde, A. (1988) *A Burst of Light: Essays*. Ithaca, NY: Firebrand Books.

Lorde, A. (2017) *The Master's Tools Will Never Dismantle the Master's House*. London: Penguin.

Lyle, K. (2017) 'Addressing race inequality in Scotland: The way forward'. Online. https://docs.wixstatic.com/ugd/7ec2e5_c04fc96855ca4eff8284c48a6939fa41.pdf (accessed 12 January 2020).

Mirza, H.S. (2006) '"Race", gender and educational desire'. *Race Ethnicity and Education*, 9 (2), 137–58. Online. doi: 10.1080/13613320600696623 (accessed 12 January 2020).

Mirza, H.S. (2015) 'Decolonizing higher education: Black feminism and the intersectionality of race and gender'. *Journal of Feminist Scholarship*, 7–8, 1–12. Online. https://digitalcommons.uri.edu/jfs/vol7/iss7/3/ (accessed 12 January 2020).

Nnaemeka, O. and Ezeilo, J. (2005) *Engendering Human Rights: Cultural and socio-economic realities in Africa*. New York: Palgrave Macmillan.

Oloo, H., Wanjiru, M. and Newell-Jones, K. (2011) *Female Genital Mutilation in Kenya: The role of alternative rights of passage; A case study in the Kisii and Kuria districts*.

Scottish Government (2015) 'Community Empowerment (Scotland) Act: A summary'. Online. www.gov.scot/publications/community-empowerment-scotland-act-summary/ (accessed 12 January 2020).

Scottish Government (2016) 'Responding to female genital mutilation: Multi-agency guidance'. Online. www.gov.scot/publications/responding-female-genital-mutilation-fgm-scotland-multi-agency-guidance-978-1-78851-364-7/pages/4/ (accessed 12 January 2020).

Scottish Government (2017) 'Addressing race inequality in Scotland: The way forward'. Online. https://docs.wixstatic.com/ugd/7ec2e5_c04fc96855ca4eff8284c48a6939fa41.pdf (accessed 12 January 2020).

Ima Jackson

Strang, A., Baillot, H. and Mignard, E. (2016) *Rights, Resilience and Refugee Integration in Scotland: New Scots & the holistic integration service*. Online. https://tinyurl.com/y988mtrp (accessed 29 March 2017).

Toubia, N. (1994) 'Female circumcision as a public health issue'. *New England Journal of Medicine*, 331 (11), 712–16.

Walley, J. (1997) 'Searching for "voices": Feminism, anthropology, and the global debate over female genital operations'. *Cultural Anthropology*, 12 (3), 405–38.

Walsh, D., Duncan, B., Fischbacher, C., Douglas, A., Erdman, J., McCartney, G., Norman, P. and Whyte, B. (2019) 'Increasingly diverse: The changing ethnic profiles of Scotland and Glasgow and the implications for population health'. *Applied Spatial Analysis and Policy*, 12 (4), 983–1009. Online. https://doi.org/10.1007/s12061-018-9281-7 (accessed 12 January 2020).

Wasige, J. and Jackson, I. (2018) 'Female genital mutilation: A form of gender-based violence'. In Lombard, N. (ed.) *The Routledge Handbook of Gender and Violence*. London: Routledge, 196–207. Online. doi: 10.4324/9781315612997 (accessed 12 January 2020).

Zimunya, M. (2019) 'Considering racism as a fundamental cause of health inequality'. Paper presented at the Glasgow Centre for Population Health, Glasgow, 18 April.

Chapter 5

Tackling racism and racial inequality in social work education and practice

Josephine Kwhali

This chapter is dedicated to my daughter and grandchildren, in whose lives the past is reflected and in whose faces the future is envisaged.

Introduction

This chapter is a reflective analysis of my personal involvement in initiatives to address racism and racial inequality in social work education and practice. I highlight my contributions over the years and the personal and professional challenges I encountered. I have focused largely on London, where considerable numbers of African Caribbean people reside and where the headquarters of the Central Council for Education and Training in Social Work (CCETSW) is located. My chapter draws on Black womanist literature through which my own consciousness was incrementally raised, while also acknowledging the work of Black male and White feminist writers and theorists who have been key in informing my theoretical understandings of class, race and gender. In 1989 the CCETSW issued the following policy statement:

> Racism is endemic in the values, attitudes and structure of British society, including those of social services and social work education. CCETSW recognises that the effects of racism on Black people are incompatible with the values of social work and therefore seeks to combat racist practices in all areas of its responsibilities. (Cited in CCETSW (1989: amended 1991): 46)

Two years later it published rules and requirements for the qualifying Diploma in Social Work (DipSW). This includes the need for social work students to understand the processes of structural oppression, to work in ethnically sensitive ways and to demonstrate an awareness of individual and institutional racism and 'ways to combat both through anti-racist practice' (CCETSW, 1991a: 16). Education institutions and practice settings are expected to provide learning environments where students are assisted in understanding and addressing various forms of discrimination. For readers with lived experience of racism and its effects, these regulations may not appear contentious. Yet 35 years later, racism does not feature in the profession's draft standards, which exclude any mention of racism or structural inequality. Nor do they require students to demonstrate any skills in applying knowledge of racial inequality in their interventions.

In this chapter I aim to highlight what can be achieved when enough people are committed to change, while demonstrating its tentative nature when dominant group interests are threatened. Higher education students do not exist in isolation from the professional roles they may subsequently occupy or the communities in which they reside. I have endeavoured to highlight how the momentum for change emerged from outside the academy, and highlight the impact of partnerships that embraced community activists, local politicians, practitioners, managers and educators. My chapter is a personal narrative that explores my own growing consciousness through the duality of theoretical knowledge and practice wisdom combined with my continuing exposure to racism. Bruner (1986) argues that different ways of knowing, viewing knowledge and the knower are interdependent with narratives embedded within history, context, culture, language, experience and understandings. Personal experiences such as poverty and unemployment are inextricably linked with wider social and political inequalities and are relevant in understanding racism and racial inequality from a sociological perspective (Wright Mills, 1959). Black feminist theory exposes the role gender plays in social inequality. For example, hooks (1994) theorized her experiences as a Black girl constrained by gender ideologies and came to understand them in the context of segregation, racism and the societal constraints imposed on both Black men and women, while Hill Collins (1990) argues that the differing perspectives that Black women articulate through interconnecting experiences of racism, sexism, class and economic oppression provide unique epistemological insights.

My chapter is written from the perspective of a solitary Black woman whose knowledge emerges from the pit of racial oppression. Yet, I am one of thousands in colleges, universities and professions across the UK who understands what it is to be derogated, misinterpreted and to see their efforts marginalized and criticized. I am one among thousands who have seen their motives trashed, who walk the weary path between trying to effect change and endlessly explaining why such change is important, while simultaneously feeling under pressure to conform, fit in and shut up. Racism is no respecter of age, generation or geographical location. My testimony in this chapter, in its essence if not in detail, will surely find resonance with many of my sisters (and hopefully brothers) who are making their own individual and collective contributions.

Setting the context for the stirring of change

My early days in social work were characterized by racial isolation. I was the only Black student on my social work training course and on other qualifying programmes that preceded it. My colour was viewed as irrelevant by course tutors, which was demeaning, given that a core element of my upbringing and identity was being denied and the crude racism shaped by childhood experiences negated. Like others of my generation, Black children were growing up during the 1960s and '70s in an atmosphere of unbridled racism. This included the Tory candidate Peter Griffiths' 1964 election campaign slogan: 'If you want a n****r for a neighbour vote Labour' (Yemm, 2016) and MP Enoch Powell's 1968 'Rivers of Blood' speech, which claimed that the 'influx' of Black and Asian immigrants 'flooding' London and the Midlands would lead to a race war, with the 'Black man' eventually having the upper hand over the 'White man' (Telegraph, 2007).

Rose's (1969) five-year study of British race relations identified largely pejorative and disapproving attitudes towards Black citizens with the formal rhetoric of equality far removed from the realities of Black people's daily lives and the entrenched racism they experienced. In Milner's (1975) work, White children described Black children as 'stinky', 'no good' or used phrases such as 'he kills people' or 'I don't like him, he's a blackie'. Coard (1971) highlights the reluctance of Black children to acknowledge his or their own Blackness, and their emotional struggles to reconcile the reality of their colour with the name calling and racist stereotypes to which they were subjected. He argues that Black people were not passive recipients of such overt racism and, despite the discrimination they faced, many went on to make significant contributions to the professions they entered and to the challenging of racism within colleges and universities. Looking back, there was little option. I could not stand apart from the issues faced by Black people because I was one of them and subject to the same racism and its erosion of one's humanity. I lived and worked in inner cities in both London and the Midlands where I witnessed Black children trying to scrub off their colour and being told to ignore the racial insults to which they were exposed. 'Coloured' children, as they were then referred to, were over-represented in care, especially those of dual Black/White parentage (Rowe and Lambert, 1973). Eighty per cent of White foster carers refused to take 'coloured' children, who were generally viewed as both undesirable and hard to place (Patterson cited in Kirton,

2000). According to Raynor (1970: 68), those willing to adopt such children were required to exhibit 'no more than a minimal amount of mild prejudice' with no indication as to what constituted 'mild prejudice', how it might be assessed or by whom.

Like other Black people, I entered social work because we wanted to make a difference to children in need and through our own lived experiences of racism to ensure a different reality for Black children. When I attended further education, I listened to educators and practitioners disparaging Black family life and exhibiting little understanding of the challenges Black parents faced. I claimed no expertise and rejected the implicit assumption that being Black of itself meant that an individual would be a positive advocate against racism or could speak for people of colour collectively. What I did have was an abhorrence of racism in its blatant and more 'benign' forms, and personal experience of knowing its destructive force on the identity, self-worth and self-esteem of Black children and adults. I was determined to be part of the process of change.

Knowledge as action and action as knowledge

When I returned to London in the mid-1980s, actions were already being initiated within social work and these provided the foundations for my own involvement and contribution. In 1983, New Black Families (NBF) was established and helped build on the success of the 1975 Soul Kids Campaign in finding Black foster and adoptive families for Black children. Under the directorship of John Small, a British Jamaican who went on to become one of the first Black directors of social services, NBF challenged the dominant narrative regarding the placement of Black children in White families. Small (1984: 129) argued that 'the one-way traffic of Black children into White families begs fundamental questions of power and ideology. It raises questions as to the type of relationship that exists between Blacks and Whites, and furthermore, the type of society those involved in the practice are creating.' Small criticized Gill and Jackson's research (1983) in concluding that trans-racial adoption was a 'success' despite the Black children denying their racial background and having been 'made White in all but skin colour' (cited in Small, 1984: 129). Small posited that 'White children in substitute or natural families do not deny that they are White or want to be Black. Gill and Jackson have tried to disguise the most vital issue confronting the society at present' (1984: 129).

In 1983, Small established the Association of Black Social Workers and Allied Professions (ABSWAP) and was its first president. Penny Pennie spoke of the organization's determination to recruit Black foster and adoptive carers in light of the local authority's previous indifference, explaining the need to build relationships with the communities:

> We began at the grassroots. We went to black churches. We asked…
> what kinds of help they wanted from the council before we would
> talk to them about the needs of black children. We organized
> information meetings in black churches after the Sunday service
> and created a network to communicate information amongst the
> congregations. (Pennie, 2019)

The work of pioneers such as Small and Pennie demonstrated the importance of embedding initiatives designed to benefit Black people in communities and gain legitimacy for their actions. Through their practice-based work and theoretical insights they demonstrated an understanding of the political and historical context within which decisions about Black children's welfare were made and the embedded racism that denied Black people agency for their own children. These points were important for my own learning – that social and political knowledge is not just gained within the academy and neither should it remain there if change is to speak to the concerns and experiences of the anticipated beneficiaries. On a practical level it meant that a number of us within the same and neighbouring authorities were able to undertake a range of interconnecting actions. Hence, when I was a middle manager, I was involved in many practice initiatives, recognizing that professional practice and the values and assumptions that underpin it could not be separated from the education and training received by its current and future practitioners.

Within and beyond the academy

I had the dubious advantage of being in a middle management position with responsibility for day-care services for children in need. Eighty-five per cent of the children assessed as 'in need' were Black British with the majority being children of parents working in low-paid jobs and struggling with the practical consequences of poverty and poor housing. Their need was for better-paid work, improved housing and less drudgery. In his research, Van Der Eyken (1984) exposed how poverty and social exclusion became intertwined with social problems when assessing families' eligibility for social services-funded day care: primarily stigmatizing Black children and poor White families. Sadly, little has changed given the four UK nations research by Morris *et al.*, (2018), which demonstrated the link between social deprivation and social work interventions. The almost exclusively White staff were ill-equipped through their training to understand the experiences of inner-city Black parents, the identity needs of small Black children, or community unrest. They had all undertaken the two-year Nursery Nursing Examination Board (NNEB) qualification straight from school at the ages of 16 or 17; the same qualification obtained by those who wished to become private nannies or to work as nursery nurses in special care baby units or under teachers in nursery schools. Prior to entering social work, I had obtained the qualification myself. While it had many strengths with its focus on child development and the practical care of babies and infants, it had a number of deficiencies, notably the lack of focus on issues of social deprivation, child protection, rejection and loss, structural inequality or the development needs of any group of children who were not White and able-bodied.

Unqualified day-care assistants were predominantly Black and resented having no opportunity for promotion to qualified and more senior roles, despite frequently being older than the nursery nurses and managers, having children of their own and wide-ranging experiences and qualifications in nursing, youth work, residential and related roles. While Black parents appreciated the care provided, the majority felt in discussions with me that the qualified staff were disproportionately young, had limited life experience, lived outside inner London and knew little of the daily realities experienced by Black individuals and families. They were also critical of the dearth of positive Black role models and toys, books and educational materials that failed to represent the diversity of the children attending the centres. With the support of committee and service users, recruitment to practitioner and manager posts would no longer be limited to NNEB holders but widened out to accredit prior experience and qualifications. In addition, the training department developed a wide-ranging internal education and training day-release programme available to existing staff and mandatory for those entering the work with rather limited experience of child development. Proposals were made for supporting and seconding staff onto social work qualifying programmes, both to widen knowledge and expertise within the day-care service itself and to provide promotional opportunities within the service and across other areas of social work practice.

I was not a lone maverick, single-handedly driving through policy, but a contributor to concerted efforts of individuals across practice, educational and community settings, combined with the commitment of key Black local politicians and community activists to effect change. Equally, any significant and far-reaching change requires inside champions committed to seeing a development through and who are willing and able to manage the almost inevitable negativity that occurs when the interests of majority groups are challenged. I was fortunate enough to be in that role. However, I did not anticipate the impact increased numbers of Black staff in my own service and others would have on social work qualifying courses.

Whose knowledge, whose truth and whose experience?

Before reflecting on how Paper 30 (CCETSW, 1989; amended 1991) emerged within social work education and training and the nature of the reaction, I wish to explore the role of knowledge and truth in the process. When Hudson and Williams (2016) identify the long struggle for academic freedom in pursuit of truth and the advancement of knowledge, the question is posed: Whose truth and whose knowledge? I had spent my entire formal education reading about, hearing from and being taught by White people. Had I not known differently I might have concluded that White people discovered everything, invented everything, wrote everything and represented the uncontested and definitive position on civilization and human progress. However, my experiences of racism and sexism gave me insights that there were multiple truths on history and the colonial and postcolonial relationship between White people and those of colour. I needed to pursue truth in ways that spoke to my lived experiences and I needed theory to guide my actions and understand those of the generations who walked before me in the advancement of Black humanity.

Reaching a more informed understanding of race and gender has been a series of building blocks in challenging what I thought I knew, shifting my world view, informing my teaching, research and practice and politicizing my consciousness as a Black woman in a White majority society. While I have benefited enormously from the insights of Black women writers and womanist theory, such writings have often developed as a counter-narrative to the exclusion of Black women's perspectives in the writings of White women and Black men. I have often struggled to find myself in such writings, but this does not mean that their perspectives have no theoretical value, both in their own right and in forcing me to think why my own narrative and experiences as a Black woman might be different. Eddo-Lodge (2017: 151), for instance, wrote of feminism being her 'first love' at the age of 19, with De Beauvoir's work (1949) providing her with an initial framework to understand the world and helping her to become a more critical and confident woman. As time went on, she began to critique White feminism for its antipathy to Black women and what she described as 'tiptoeing around whiteness in feminist spaces' (Eddo-Lodge, 2017: 154). She came to recognize the limitations of White feminism and her theoretical and emotional need to integrate gender and race as intrinsic parts of her whole self.

My initial exposure to race theory was through the work of the W.E.B Du Bois (1994) and his arguments on the problem of the 'color line', not simply as a national and personal question but in its larger world aspect in time and space' (1994: 47). In *The Souls of Black Folk* (1994, original publication 1903) Du Bois expands his thinking, arguing that race is a socio-bio construct used to legitimate the subjugation of Black people and the dominance of Whites. He located the oppression of Black people in the wider context of inequality of power, believing that the 'Black man' [sic] would find ways to resist. He also introduced the concept of 'double consciousness' whereby Black people are forced to view themselves through the dominant perspectives of White people. As such perspectives are largely negative and rooted in slavery, colonialism, oppression and contempt, this creates an internal conflict for Black people. They are aware of the largely negative ways in which they are viewed and spoken of while being required to construct a more positive and internalized sense of self for their own psychological wellbeing. Frantz Fanon (1986, original publication 1952) also explored the notion of double-consciousness, focusing on the psychology of colonialism and its internalization by the colonized who often see themselves through the eyes of their oppressors and unconsciously assimilate into Eurocentric social norms.

It was Toni Morrison's *The Bluest Eye* (1970) that brought these theoretical insights to life for me. It tells the story of a young girl, Pecola, who yearns for her eyes to turn blue so that she will be as loved and considered as beautiful as the blonde-haired White girls whom she envies. That story is also my story and the story of the dozens of Black women and children with whom I have worked – who have been insulted for our colour (too Black or not Black enough), called racist names, subjected to powerful images of White beauty and flowing blonde locks, from which Black women were historically excluded. The blend of Fanon and Du Bois's intellectual theory combined with auto-ethnographic writings by Morrison (1970), Selvon (1956) and Emecheta (1974, 1976, 1977, 1979) linked the head with the heart and created a yearning for further knowledge that integrated aspects of gender, class and racialized experiences.

The term intersectionality was initially theorized by Kimberlé Crenshaw (1989) who argued how the intertwining of race and gender power created the bias, violence and discrimination perpetuated against Black women. However, I became aware of the interlink between race, class and gender through hooks's work. I was also influenced by the writings of Angela Davis (1982, 1984) who positioned Black women as central to the struggle for gender equality, and the painful poignancy of Alice Walker's (1983) and Maya Angelou's books and poems (1969, 1978). Black feminist literature allowed me to locate myself emotionally and intellectually as a Black woman within a broader yearning for race, gender and class equality. It was this incremental emergence of the knowing with the feeling and the doing that enabled me to better understand issues of identity and the weary struggle of dealing with everyday outcomes of intersectional inequality and the double-consciousness theorized by Fanon and Du Bois. In so doing I also came to understand and learn to counteract the arrogant way in which Black people's concerns and perspectives were often dismissed and White dominance sustained. In Lorde's words:

> those of us who have been forged in the crucibles of difference – those of us who are poor, who are lesbians, who are Black, who are older – know that survival is not an academic skill. It is learning how to take our differences and make them strengths. (Lorde, 1981)

Social work education towards critical race theory

Along with a number of other Black managers and small numbers of Black educators, I was increasingly perturbed by the experiences of Black staff attending social work courses from my own authority and beyond. It was evident that differences were not viewed as strengths. Students spoke of some White students being resentful of their presence; a curriculum that excluded any consideration of ethnic, religious and cultural diversity; educators who resented any challenge to dominant truths; and disproportionate failure rates on placements where Black students felt unsupported by both tutors and practice educators. As Ely and Denny (1987: 199), two White academics, commented in relation to race: 'The pattern of discrimination and disadvantage is reproduced and reinforced within the operations of social work rather than being compensated by its provision.'

At a conference on social work education and training (Mickleton Conference, 1987), I and a number of Black attendees actively challenged CCETSW to address the experiences of Black students on social work courses and the lack of acknowledgement given to issues of racism, sexism and other inequalities. Before the next CCETSW conference we contacted the Black academics, managers, students and staff known to us and encouraging them to attend. At this conference CCETSW's inaction on inequalities was being largely justified with promises of sweeteners in the future if we swallowed the sour lemon today. As a group of approximately thirty Black individuals we collectively walked out midway through, explaining that we needed time and space to talk with each other, to share experiences and to strategize.

Under such pressure, CCETSW subsequently established the Black Perspectives Committee (BPC). In conjunction with BPC, the Black external examiners' group and Black practice educators (of which I was a member), a number of projects were initiated by CCETSW (CCETSW, 1991b; Local Government Management Board, 1991) designed to enhance the teaching of anti-racism in Diploma in Social Work programmes and improve practice learning by drawing on the experiences of Black and Asian academics, practitioners and managers. The work included initiatives to support Black practice educators and to encourage social work education providers to involve experienced Black practitioners and managers as external examiners on their courses. I undertook such a role within a number of higher education institutions and in many cases academic staff were responsive to my contributions. Many were able to make links between their own commitment to such issues of gender, sexuality, and disability and, more broadly, to equality and human rights that underpinned social work values.

The local authority that I worked in continued to second staff to an educational institution that disproportionately failed Black students and was resistant even to discussing staffing and curriculum changes, never mind implementing them. Excessive time was taken up in meetings with academic staff, liaising with disgruntled students and advocating for those experiencing the worst excesses of poor treatment. Additionally, the programme was also failing White students who were ill-equipped to understand complex issues of poverty, neglect and family dysfunction in both White and Black communities and its implications for the safety and protection of children. In conjunction with a supportive White training officer and another Black manager we charted the experiences of Black students, their exam and essay grades, their experiences on placement and aspects of the curriculum that were unhelpful for equipping staff for practice. We then held discussions with another higher education provider who was generally well regarded by neighbouring authorities and recommended to the committee that we transferred our business to them, while advising self-funding social work students on the merits and demerits of different courses. When the BPC and CCETSW stated that 'racism was endemic in the values, attitudes and structures of British society', those of us involved in the struggle for racial equality felt that the words represented a culmination of all that we, our parents and forefathers and mothers had lived through for decades. The stereotypes applied to us, the insults we endured, our absence from education curricula, the jobs we were denied, the children whose needs were not met, the young people criminalized and problematized; the indignities of stop and search; the poverty lived and a history in which we had been enslaved, colonized and humiliated. To us the statement represented our lived reality.

To their credit, CCETSW listened to our voices and our truth, understood something of our pain and of the need for change. They responded accordingly, expressing in their statement theoretical ideas that had academic validity nearly twenty years ago. Unfortunately, few in social work education, the government or the media appeared to have engaged with this theory. If they had they were dismissive and, in some cases, indignant at any suggestion that racism and structural inequality existed and that its teaching was a matter for social work education and training. In her work on White identity (Helms and Carter, 1990), Janet Helms argues that many White people are initially oblivious to racism, deny the relevance of skin colour and feel that the very discussion of racial difference creates the problem. When confronted by Black people's experiences or evidence of the historical, structural and contemporary privileging of Whiteness they may shift to a position of guilt, embarrassment and shame. According to Helms, such guilt might be replaced by a mentality that blames the victim, rejecting lived experiences and locating the negativity of Black people's experiences in their own failings, while justifying any White privileges as deserved or achieved through hard work. It is only in the final stages of Helm's model that White people can retain a secure sense of self while understanding Whiteness in the context of racial injustice and therefore acknowledging racism and becoming supporters of change.

Action and reaction: The White backlash

In 1992 the *Times* criticized CCETSW's alleged 'obsession' with 'ologies' and 'isms', with Tim Yeo, then junior Conservative Health Minister, reminding CCETSW of its need to 'deliver value for money and real measurable achievement' (Yeo, 1992). With the shift from publicly provided services to private providers following the NHS and Community Care Act 1991, Yeo wrote that CCETSW needed to ensure 'that training fully prepares social workers for their new roles within the mixed economy of care', which 'required management skills and a clear understanding of budgetary issues' (Yeo, 1992: 2). Writing in the *Observer* in 1993, under the heading 'Oppressive urge to stop oppression', Melanie Phillips criticized anti-racist education for its 'authoritarian tendencies and [being] counter to principles of freedom of thought'. In addition, Bryan Appleyard, writing in the *Independent* in 1993, claimed that 'A significant number of social work courses have been poisoned by Paper 30-inspired political correctness, and in those courses serious teaching and free debate can be said to be impossible.' Appleyard said that CCETSW had 'elevated racism to a national epidemic' and he was especially vociferous in his criticism of CCETSW's concern over the endemic nature of racism. He suggested that in 'world terms' British society was 'relatively free of racist tension and, historically, it was the British rather than the equally implicated Arabs and Africans who abolished the slave trade, so we might reasonably congratulate ourselves on being the most anti-racist culture on earth'. Hence, not only were Black people implicitly criticized for having the temerity to articulate a different discourse regarding racism within higher education, but the history of the transatlantic slave trade is reframed from one in which the British were the major initiators, perpetrators and beneficiaries (Williams, 1944; Walvin, 1993) to a story where they alone are the undisputed saviours and that economics and slave rebellions played no part (Ryden, 2009).

Essentially, the attack was not on CCETSW, who had done little more than respond to Black people's concerns, but on Black workers, educators and students themselves. Our perceived threatening Black voices needed to be silenced because of our audacity in challenging social work education and its claim to truth. Myself and others who were part of the process of change knew that our truths were being negated and our history trashed. We knew that the perspectives articulated by Black theorists were being ignored – if they were even known of – and that the experiences of Black educators, practitioners and service users did not count. We had to relearn that were we were in the profession under sufferance. The learning that emerged '*Out of the huts of history's shame / Up from a past that's rooted in pain*' (Angelou, 1978) counted for little; the words of bell hooks on the devaluation of Black womanhood were etched in the condemning voices of writers such as Robert Pinker (1993) and Appleyard, secure in their largely uncontested White, male privilege. We Black women had to know our place and dispense with any notion that we had the right to challenge the establishment's liberal and benevolent view of itself. It felt personal because it was demonstrating anew the numerous platforms and outlets on which White commentators could articulate and publicize their views while we who were Black had to spend years and infinite energy coercing those with influence to make small changes that could then be flicked aside with contempt.

During a speech at a 1994 Commons debate, the Conservative Secretary of State for Health Virginia Bottomley responded to a fellow MP's question on CCETSW's alleged 'political correctness' thus:

> There can be no place in the training of social workers for politically correct notions, for the domination of ideology and textbook theories over practical skills for children. Social workers have an important job to do, and their decisions should not be informed by fashionable theories, but by sensible, time-honoured principles and values. (Bottomley, 1994)

The idea that universities and colleges should not teach 'textbook theories' was itself interesting and implied that 'practical skills' required no research or theory regarding their effectiveness. I assumed, then and now, that the only 'politically correct notions' were those that reinforced the 'principles and values' of Bottomley and other White political, academic and media figures who were outraged by Paper 30's supposed contents. Critically, the statement simply accepted journalists' criticisms when any neutral observer could see that the regulations paid detailed attention to 'practical skills'; not least when students spent nearly 50 per cent of the course on social work practice placements.

The outcome of this backlash was that Tony Hall was replaced as CCETSW's director and a number of the race 'initiatives', including the BPC, disbanded. Paper 30 and the qualifying requirements were reviewed in 1994. According to Weinstein (2014), 'the review aroused cynicism and a reluctance to advocate for something that many stakeholders felt was a sell-out'. I organized a group of Black practitioners, managers and educators in critiquing the review draft and the lack of consultation on its content. Paper 30 was, however, amended and reference to 'endemic racism' removed. CCETSW was abolished in 2001 and its successor body made no mention of racism, sexism, homophobia or structural inequality.

Lessons to be learned

In my concluding reflections I once again return to the words of Audre Lorde:

> For the master's tools will never dismantle the master's house. They may allow us to temporarily beat him at his own game, but they will never enable us to bring about genuine change. Racism and homophobia are real conditions of all our lives in this place and time. I urge each one of us here to reach down into that deep place of knowledge inside herself and touch that terror and loathing of any difference that lives here. See whose face it wears. Then the personal as the political can begin to illuminate all our choices. (Lorde, 1981: 112)

Lorde's theory can be applied to my experience as recounted in this chapter, showing that micro changes that do not alter the status quo are acceptable but that any initiatives that challenge structural inequality and allow Black people agency will be challenged, reframed and eliminated, such as that which occurred in response to Paper 30. Within social work education there has been an incremental acceptance of the need for ethnically sensitive social work or cultural competence (Laird, 2008; Rothman, 2008), terms that are poorly defined as differing cultures that exist within a single ethnic group as well as across them. This means the specifics of race and racism can be ignored, reducing complex issues to a set of skills to be acquired, and justifying the trashing of any perspective that centralizes Black people's lived experiences and historical understandings of oppression. Criticisms have been made of anti-racism both as a theoretical concept and as a practice (Lentin, 2000). I believe there is an urgent need to address the suffering of Black children and families mired in poverty, trans-racially placed, disparaged and marginalized in schools and colleges. Hence it is important to remain focused on the objectives of change and not merely to become mired in theoretical attempts to find universal agreement for terms that are socially constructed.

In the universities where I taught, 30–50 per cent of social work students were from visible minority groups. While many complained endlessly about racism they did very little to challenge it, simply wanting to secure degrees or promotion, believing that they could ignore racism as long as they conformed, played the game and criticized the actions of other individuals or aspects of their cultural heritage in front of their White peers. As academics I believe it important that we spend less time attempting to persuade some of our White counterparts to be more just and focus our attention on decolonizing each other's thinking and not merely the curriculum. As Lorde argues:

> Black and Third World people are expected to educate white people as to our humanity. Women are expected to educate men. Lesbians and gay men are expected to educate the heterosexual world. The oppressors maintain their position and evade their responsibility for their own actions. There is a constant drain of energy which might be better used in redefining ourselves and devising realistic scenarios for altering the present and constructing the future. (Lorde, 2007: 115)

In reading the works of White academics on anti-racism and observing their cerebral and detached engagement from within the Ivory Tower, I might wonder why those of us who lived it have been rendered largely invisible in the story. As initiatives have been dismantled and the overt commitment of social work to issues of justice and equality diluted, the reader might ask if it was all worth it. My answer is yes, it was worth it, for many reasons. Social work education has not entirely retreated from considerations of race and gender. As Singh (2011) stated, there is now a wide body of literature on questions of culture, diversity, and anti-discriminatory and anti-oppressive practice. Weinstein (2014) suggests that 'Social Work values were rediscovered and modernized with new theories of empowering service users and working in partnership'. From my own experience I know there to be people of good will who understand the importance of ensuring that students are equipped not only to understand issues of race, gender and structural inequality but also to take that understanding into their own lives and practice.

Most importantly, I and others involved in the changes before and after Paper 30 stayed in the profession and were spread out across the country. We took the knowledge gained from our experience into professional, managerial and academic roles. My theoretical learning informed my teaching and research, my racial learning informed my work with Black students, colleagues, staff and service users, and my personal learning gave me the courage and tenacity to keep going. In so doing we opened up employment, promotional and educational opportunities for Black staff previously denied them, which enabled us and them to contribute to the profession beyond the specific confines of race. We enhanced the learning of many White colleagues while upsetting many others. We forged strong friendships that endure to this day and gained much from each other. We made mistakes and were sometimes unduly harsh on ourselves and each other – but we had no template, only youthful energy and the painful scars of racism that spurred us on.

The incremental nature of racial change is such that we have to build upon and learn from our experiences even if an initiative in a given space and time did not eliminate deeply institutionalized inequalities or achieve as much as we might have hoped. No matter how much we struggle, are derogated, denied, marginalized, misinterpreted and ignored, the pain we endure is far less than those who have struggled before us against colonialism, slavery and segregation. I owe a debt of life and gratitude to those who went before me. If we simply give up and fail to act, then the comfortable lives and fancy job titles of the few will have been gained from the sacrifices and subjugation of the many.

References

Angelou, M. (1969) *I Know Why the Caged Bird Sings*. New York: Random House.

Angelou, M. (1978) *And Still I Rise*. New York: Random House.

Appleyard, B. (1993) 'Why paint so black a picture? A social work directive elevates racism to a national epidemic. It is a national disgrace'. *The Independent*, 4 August.

Bottomley, V. (1984) cited in Hansard. January 1994: Volume 236 cc146–7.

Bruner, J. (1986) Actual Minds, Possible Worlds. Cambridge, MA: Harvard University Press.

CCETSW (Central Council for Education and Training in Social WorK) (1989: amended 1991) *DipSW Rules and Requirements for the Diploma in Social Work, Paper 30*. London: CCETSW.

CCETSW (Central Council for Education and Training in Social Work) (1991a) *One Small Step Towards Racial Justice*. London: CCETSW.

CCETSW (Central Council for Education and Training in Social Work) (1991b) *Setting the Context for Change*. Leeds: CCETSW/Northern CD Project.

Coard, B. (1971) *How the West Indian Child is Made Educationally Sub-normal in the British School System: The scandal of the black child in schools in Britain*. London: New Beacon Books.

Crenshaw, K. (1989) 'Demarginalizing the intersection of race and sex: A black feminist critique of antidiscrimination doctrine, feminist theory and anti-racist politics'. *University of Chicago Legal Forum*, 1 (8), Volume 1989.

Davis, A. (1982) *Women, Race and Class*. London: Women's Press.

Davis, A. (1984) *Women, Culture and Politics*. London: Women's Press.

De Beauvoir, S. (1949) *The Second Sex*. Trans. Borde, C. and Malovany-Chevallier, S. London: Penguin Random House.

Du Bois, W.E.B. (1994) *The Souls of Black Folk*. New York: Dover.

Eddo-Lodge, R. (2017) *Why I'm No Longer Talking to White People About Race*. London: Bloomsbury.

Ely, P. and Denny, D. (1987) *Social Work in a Multiracial Society*. London: Gower.

Emecheta, B. (1974) *Second Class Citizen*. London: Allison and Busby.

Emecheta, B. (1976) *The Bride Price*. New York: George Braziller.

Emecheta, B. (1977) *The Slave Girl*. London: Allison and Busby.

Emecheta, B. (1979) *The Joys of Motherhood*. London: Allison and Busby.

Fanon, F. (1986) *Black Skin, White Masks*. London: Pluto Classics.

Gill, O. and Jackson, B. (1983) *Adoption and Race: Black, Asian and mixed race children in white families*. London: Batsford.

Helms, J.E. and Carter, R.T. (1990) 'Development of the white racial identity inventory'. In Helms, J.E. (ed.), *Black and White Racial Identity: Theory, research and practice*. Westport, CT: Greenwood Press, 67–80.

Hill Collins, P. (1990) *Black Feminist Thought: Knowledge, consciousness and the politics of empowerment*. New York: Unwin Hyman.

hooks, b. (1994) *Teaching to Transgress: Education as the practice of freedom*. London: Routledge.

Hudson, C. and Williams, J. (eds) (2016) *Why Academic Freedom Matters: A response to current challenges*. London: Civitas.

Kirton, D. (2000) *'Race', Ethnicity and Adoption*. Buckingham: Open University Press.

Laird, S. (2008) *Anti-oppressive Social Work: A guide for developing cultural competence*. Thousand Oaks, CA: Sage.

Lentin, A. (2000) '"Race", racism, anti-racism: Challenging contemporary classifications'. *Social Identities*, (6) 1, 91–106.

Local Government Management Board with Kwhali, J. and Mukherjee, T. (1991) *The Unequal Challenge*. LGMB.

Lorde, A. (1981) 'The master's tools will never dismantle the master's house'. In Moraga, C. and Anzaldúa, G. (eds) *This Bridge Called My Back: Writings by radical women of color*. Watertown, MA: Persephone Press; 4th ed. Albany: SUNY Press, 2015.

Lorde, A. (2007) *Sister Outsider: Essays and speeches by Audre Lorde*. Berkeley, CA: Crossing Press.

Mickleton Conference (1987) cited in *Community Care Magazine: Education and Training* (March 2000). Online. www.communitycare.co.uk/2000/03/22/paperwork/ (accessed 12 January 2020).

Milner, D. (1975) *Children and Race*. London: Penguin.

Morris, K., Mason, W., Bywaters, P., Mirza, N., Brady, G., Bunting, L., Hooper, J., Scourfield, J. and Webb, C. (2018) 'Social work, poverty and child welfare interventions'. *Child and Family Social Work*, 23 (3), 364–72.

Morrison, T. (1970) *The Bluest Eye*. New York: Holt, Rinehart and Winston.

Pennie, P. (2019) cited in 'Celebrating Soul Workers'. Online. https://corambaaf.org.uk/updates/celebrating-soul-workers (accessed 12 January 2020).

Pinker, R. (1993) 'A lethal kind of looniness'. *Times Higher Educational Supplement*, 10 September.

Phillips, M. (1993) 'Oppressive urge to stop oppression'. *Observer*, 1 August.

Raynor, L. (1970) *Adoption of Non-White Children*. London: Allen and Unwin.

Rose, E.R.B. (1969) *Colour and Citizenship: A report on British race relations*. London: Oxford University Press.

Rothman, J.C. (2008) *Cultural Competence in Process and Practice: Building bridges*. Boston: Pearson.

Rowe, J. and Lambert, L. (1973) *Children Who Wait: A study of children needing substitute families*. London: Association of British Adoption Agencies.

Ryden, D.B. (2009) *West Indian Slavery and British Abolition, 1783–1807*. Cambridge: Cambridge University Press.

Selvon, S. (1956) *The Lonely Londoners*. London: Longman.

Singh, G. (2011). *Black and Minority Ethnic (BME) Students' Participation and Success in Higher Education: Improving retention and success – a synthesis of research evidence*. York: Higher Education Academy. Online. https://tinyurl.com/v6u47c4 (accessed 15 April 2020).

Small, J. (1984) 'The crisis in adoption'. *International Journal of Social Psychiatry*, 30 (1–2), 129–42.

The Telegraph (2007) 'Enoch Powell's "Rivers of Blood" speech'. *Telegraph*. Online. www.telegraph.co.uk/comment/3643823/Enoch-Powells-Rivers-of-Blood-speech.html (accessed 12 January 2020).

Van der Eyken (1984) *Day Nurseries in Action: A national study of local authority day nurseries in England, 1975–1983*. Bristol: Department of Child Health Research Unit, University of Bristol.

Walker, A. (1983) *In Search of Our Mother's Gardens: Womanist prose*. New York: Harcourt Brace Jovanovich.

Walvin, J. (1983) Slavery and the Slave Trade: A short illustrated history. Jackson: University Press of Mississippi.

Weinstein, J. (2014) 'CCETSW, "Institutional Racism" and the "PC Backlash"'. Online. www.kcl.ac.uk/scwru/swhn/2014/weinstein-ccetsw-institutional-racism-and-the-pc-backlash.pdf (accessed 12 January 2020).

Williams, E. (1944) Capitalism and Slavery. Chapel Hill: University of North Carolina Press.

Wright Mills, C. (1959) *The Sociological Imagination*. New York: Oxford University Press.

Yemm, R. (2016) 'Race, media and local politics: Smethwick and the 1964 General Election'. In Social History Society Annual Conference, 21–23 March 2016, Lancaster University.

Yeo, T. (1992) Minister's letter to CCETSW Chair, Prof. Berrick Saul. Department of Health, Richmond House.

Chapter 6

Critical reflections on transforming the Ivory Tower and beyond, part 1

Deborah Gabriel

As part of the political mission of the Black Sister Network to explore and articulate our experiences through counter-narratives, it is important that as participants we reflect on projects like the Ivory Tower, since the process of undertaking research as well as the outcomes is an important learning opportunity. After the publication of *Inside the Ivory Tower* by Trentham Books in 2017 (for convenience IT1), the seven book launches, the reader survey, reviews and press interviews, our reflections and analysis of the project influenced my decision to develop IT2. However, we never documented how each of us were impacted by the experience of participating in the project. These critical reflections therefore serve two important objectives. The first is to facilitate our individual growth through self-analysis, examining how the process of taking part in a Black feminist research project contributes to our empowerment and to stimulate ideas on how to utilize the knowledge gained. The second objective is to share our experiences to extend the impact to other women of colour, in the hope that they may be inspired by our efforts to embark on transformative projects of their own.

At the time of writing my reflection (October 2019), the Ivory Tower project was in its fifth year of existence. It has been the most rewarding, meaningful and fulfilling experience of my academic life, and the sisterhood, solidarity and sense of belonging I have found have helped sustain me through the emotionally and psychologically draining challenge of being a Black, female scholar-activist-academic in the UK higher education sector surrounded by Whiteness, privilege and extreme inequity. Maintaining my integrity and sanity have only been possible because the very real raced and gendered inequality I have experienced are what fuels my determination to tackle it. I attribute my survival to the cultivation of my 'bicultural life structure... the nucleus from which people of colour evoke the power to contest the terrain of differences that contribute to their marginal positions in White-dominated organizations' (Alfred, 2001: 123), as I argued in IT1

(Gabriel and Tate, 2017). My empowerment is driven by my connectedness to my Ivory Tower sisters and the wider Black British Academics community that is essential to my mental health and wellbeing and integral to my cultural values and heritage. This connectedness and collectivity is encapsulated in Ubuntu philosophy: *Umuntu ngumuntu ngabantu*:

> a philosophy of life, which in its most fundamental sense represents personhood, humanity, humaneness and morality; a metaphor that describes group solidarity where such group solidarity is central to the survival of communities with a scarcity of resources… which, literally translated, means a person can only be a person through others' (Xulu, 2010: 2)

It is through this connectedness that I have been able to circumvent hegemonic whiteness and re-centre myself through Black feminist research. Its subjectivity enables me to develop critical consciousness and agency, as conceptualized by Gloria Gordon (2005: 251): 'I have moved from a position of being a silent and unheard victim in the world to a place where I fully agree with Okri that "there is no such thing as a powerless people"'.

Theorizing my raced and gendered experiences is cathartic. It also facilitates critical reflection, so essential to learning, personal and intellectual growth. Desolation only occurs when oppression, marginalization, exclusion, dehumanization and objectification cannot be explained – resulting in self-deprecation. Subjectivity, critical reflection and analysis allow me to step back in a detached manner from the source of my inequality in a way that enables me to understand it and develop strategies to address it. That is how critical consciousness facilitates agency, which in turn creates self-empowerment. Black feminism is a standpoint by and for Black women and women of colour (Hill Collins, 1990) and I consider the Ivory Tower project to be significant and salient during an era where Black women continue to be undervalued in our personal and professional lives, and when the very strategies we develop to uplift ourselves – Me Too (Tarana Burke), Intersectionality (Kimberlé Crenshaw), Black Lives Matter (Alicia Garzia, Patrice Cullors, Opal Tometi) – are crudely and brazenly appropriated, often by those in positions of power and privilege who erase us in the process of elevating themselves in a way that depoliticizes the essence of our resistance.

Working with the contributors on IT2 provided an opportunity for celebrating Black Girl Magic (CaShawn Thompson); for acknowledging the determination, resilience, creativity, innovation, success and achievements of my sisters in the struggle that so often go unacknowledged and unrewarded. Reading all the chapters in this volume, and undertaking my role as editor to ensure that my sisters shine in print, has been an uplifting experience. Writing my own chapter on my 3D Pedagogy Framework was both empowering and motivating and brought a smile to my face as I reminisced on some of my joyous experiences of teaching. Even as I recollected negative moments that have marred my academic life, they became a source of empowerment as the self-reflection brought a deeper understanding of the issues and has strengthened my resolve to strive for justice and equity. I very much look forward to the next phase of the Ivory Tower project.

REFERENCES

Alfred, M.V. (2001) 'Expanding theories of career development: Adding the voices of African American women in the white academy'. *Adult Education Quarterly*, 51 (2), 108–27.

Gabriel, D. and Tate, S.A. (eds) (2017) *Inside the Ivory Tower: Narratives of women of colour surviving and thriving in British academia*. London: Trentham Books.

Gordon, G.B. (2005) 'Transforming lives: Towards bicultural competence'. In Reason, P. and Bradbury, H. (eds) *Handbook of Action Research*. London: Sage, 243–51.

Hill Collins, P. (1990) *Black Feminist Thought: Knowledge, consciousness and the politics of empowerment*. New York: Unwin Hyman.

Xulu, M. (2010) 'Ubuntu and being umuntu: Towards an ubuntu pedagogy through cultural expressions, symbolism and performance'. *Skills at Work: Theory and Practice Journal*, 3 (1), 81–7.

BARC

Building the Anti-Racist Classroom (BARC) has opened up a form of explicit political engagement with people of colour in our field. Whereas previous collaborations have revolved around co-authorship, co-organizing conference streams or one-to-one conversations, BARC is organizing workshops for consciousness-raising and community-building in non-individualistic and anti-competitive ways. Although it is informed by our own research, unlike the rest of our academic work, our work with BARC is not done for individual gain. On a personal level, each member of BARC has felt this mobilization in their own way. Our differentiated relations to White power structures shape our experiences of safety, threat, anxiety, fulfilment, satisfaction and anger (Lorde, 2018). These experiences have varied as we negotiate power; yet they are continually structured by our racialized and gendered bodies (Hill Collins, 1990). They have influenced our relationships to each other, as well as to ourselves as activists and academics, encouraging us to engage in practices of radical honesty that empower us to make principled decisions.

At a professional level, some universities and colleagues have received our work as a possible plug-in element to support diversity and inclusion programmes, identifying us as anti-racist 'professionals'. This has led to us being tokenized by some institutions (see Ahmed, 2012) but others have offered opportunities to connect and raise consciousness with extended communities of colour. From our positioning as scholar-activists working as a collective, we have been navigating uncharted territory in responding to invitations from British universities to provide consultancy, training, or bespoke workshops, and have needed to deliberate as to how the collective might evolve as an entity to accommodate them. It has been a process that some BARC members feel to be deeply problematic because it has rolled the collective's work into capitalist forms of organizing. Here, it is feared that our anti-racist politics are assimilated into commoditized or marketable elements that the university can use for increasing its own symbolic and market value without having to change internal structures. For others, the innovation can be understood as a necessary step to change the system from within. These differences within BARC almost certainly reflect the contradictions and tensions that anyone carrying out anti-racist feminist work encounters and grapples with (Anzaldúa, 1987). Though we have found no resolution, we have committed to using any profits not for individual gain but for the wider benefit of students and staff of colour. We also keep this struggle at the forefront of discussions around how we take on work, with whom we work and how we make decisions about where our activities should focus.

It has been key for us to develop and extend political relations with anti-racist feminists, Black feminists, decolonizing scholars and activists outside the business and management field. Doing so has been crucial to keeping us accountable to disciplinary debates that challenge the orthodoxies of our own field. The work has also built community among different stakeholder groups and we have managed to pool funding resources from business schools to support scholars and activists working in more precarious departments. For BARC, this has been an experiment in how resources can be redistributed in ways that centre the most marginalized students and members of staff. As such, the learning experience has presented both points of tension and growth with our various communities, be they professional or activist.

Building on the narratives and knowledge of the Ivory Tower contributors, race and gender equality initiatives must first and foremost ensure the safety of Black women and women of colour in academia. Accordingly, we propose that work addressing race equality and equity must be taken on collectively rather than individually; responses to race and gender inequality must be activated to build spaces, fund interventions, and promote ways of working that provide Black women and women of colour with support – both material and emotional (Pow, 2018; Tate, 2017). The collective work must also acknowledge that White patriarchal capitalist power co-opts movement work and re-structures itself to ensure its own reproduction and dominance. This means that anti-racist initiatives will have to be agile, and likely discreet. These must be led not only by those who spark consciousness through their intellectual work but also by those who engage in community-building that draws out love, trust and solidaristic relations among us by affirming our differences (hooks, 1995; Lorde, 2018). This is no mean feat.

While BARC refuses to accept and submit to White patriarchal capitalist modes of organizing, we are each aware of the limitations in our individual capacities to do this work. We continually remind ourselves that resting and taking refuge is just as important as showing up, committing and being clear about what each of us can offer from the margins. In the Ivory Tower project, we have seen British women of colour articulate their power to advance their agendas and build tools and techniques to create healing spaces. As the BARC collective continues and evolves, we do so in solidarity with the spirit of this work.

References

Ahmed, S. (2012) *On Being Included: Racism and diversity in institutional life.* Durham, NC: Duke University Press.

Anzaldúa G.E. (1987) *Borderlands/La Frontera: The new mestiza.* San Francisco: Aunt Lute Books.

Hill Collins, P. (1990) *Black Feminist Thought: Knowledge, consciousness and the politics of empowerment.* New York: Unwin Hyman.

hooks, b. (1995) *Killing Rage: Ending racism.* New York: Henry Holt.

Lorde, A. (2018) *The Master's Tools Will Never Dismantle the Master's House.* London: Penguin Classics.

Pow, K. (2018) '"Be exactly who you are": Black feminism in volatile political realities'. In Johnson, A., Kamunge, B. and Joseph-Salisbury, R. (eds) *The Fire Now: Anti-racist scholarship in times of explicit racial violence.* London: Zed Books, 235–49.

Tate, S.A. (2017) 'How do you feel?: "Wellbeing" as a deracinated strategic goal in UK universities'. In Gabriel, D. and Tate, S.A. (eds) *Inside the Ivory Tower: Narratives of women of colour surviving and thriving in British academia.* London: Trentham Books, 54–66.

Elizabeth Opara

When I was asked to contribute to this second book in the Ivory Tower series, I was acutely aware that I did not have a project or initiative in the traditional sense. What I did have was a continuation of my journey, which began with the writing of my chapter for *Inside the Ivory Tower* (Gabriel and Tate, 2017). The process of writing the chapter prompted self-reflection on how I practise my craft through the lens of being a Black woman scientist. I have attempted to articulate how to address barriers to STEM, specifically in academia, using acts of resistance that are driven by my own experience as a Black woman in the hope that other Black women in science might – if they have not already – begin to think about how they too can contribute to social change within the STEM landscape.

Writing this chapter has been challenging at times, primarily because the meaning and significance of the literature on gender and race took time to take hold in a way that allowed me to present my case coherently. Furthermore, as with my chapter for IT1, I made a profound connection with the literature that allowed the articulation of my strategies of resistance through the lens of my gender and race. I felt it necessary to first map out where I believe we are now when it comes to gender and race in the science academy so that it is clear to the reader that acts of resistance are imperative. I hope I have also made clear that my altruistic science identity is not focused on the need for recognition by the establishment and thus it is the root from which my roles as a science educator and mentor have broken down barriers to STEM. Although I acknowledge that the science academy, and its predominant/principal/ruling members, can be used as an instrument of change, this cannot be achieved without acts of resistance – whether in a lecture theatre, laboratory, or sitting in an office having a one-to-one with another Black woman scientist – driven by our lived experience. Resistance that is focused on the needs, wants and traditions of the science academy and the wider society that it represents is not resistance and will do little to address the domination of science by one particular group – a dominance that will be to the detriment of all scientists if it is allowed to persist.

Finally, I must acknowledge Black British Academics, especially the Black Sister Network, for my contribution. I sought out other Black academics at a time when I knew it was time for me to be among those who recognized and understood my lived experience in academia. This network first afforded me a place to heal through my contribution to IT1 and is now instrumental in the fruition of the work I describe here. It continues to compel and empower me to develop and carry out acts of resistance to overcome the exclusion and isolation I, and the Black women I talk about in this chapter, have experienced, and has given me the courage, the language and the voice to articulate these acts from a Black feminist and critical race perspective. This network, specifically the solidarity it has achieved through sisterhood, is the embodiment of the aspirational Black women's scientist network I describe in my chapter. Furthermore, this network is making it possible for this work to be read by all in the academy. In doing so it is continuing to challenge institutions to accept and understand that they must first reject their misplaced and misconceived notions of gender and race before beginning the process of engaging with women of colour on their own terms.

REFERENCES

Gabriel, D. and Tate, S.A. (eds) (2017) *Inside the Ivory Tower: Narratives of women of colour surviving and thriving in British academia*. London: Trentham Books.

Ima Jackson

The fact that there is an IT2 changes the landscape for me. Participating is an ongoing, supportive, intellectually stimulating relationship with Black female scholars who I can call on and be called on by. As virtually the lone woman of African descent in the science academy in Scotland, I have developed ways to manage the isolation, but working on IT1 and IT2 has been transformative because from the onset the space we engage in together begins with shared understanding.

In IT1 I reflected on why I connected strongly with women migrants and families of colour, and how we built research together. However, there were so many other ways I have navigated the challenges and often complex experiences that I omitted from IT1. For example, I used my PhD scholarship, although it had little connection to my overall interest, to investigate dynamics within inter-professional relationships, understand assumptions within language use in text and word, and evidence the power differentials and tensions within the accepted knowledge. I did so to identify mechanisms that denote acceptance and resistance to the dominant narratives and accepted ways of knowledge production in a clinical setting. Through reflection in IT1, I came to a greater understanding of how I later applied this approach within my own work to investigate, incorporate and gain wider acceptance and understanding of how racism and marginalization are manifested and can be understood and disrupted within our policy and research processes in Scotland.

Participating in IT2 and reframing my work within transformative social justice practice has been professionally and intellectually helpful, as well as building my personal confidence. As I am usually the only scholar of colour, I have often found it difficult to explain my thinking and the way I work, even though I have always understood it as a response to the isolated scholarly reality in which I live and work. For years I have been quietly building cross-sectoral, professional relationships with the key decision-makers on Scottish policy and practice. I have done this in order to influence, encourage and support those who wish to make change, but change that pays careful attention to racialization and racism. Participating in IT2 has supported the ongoing consolidation of that ambition.

Scotland is attempting to build itself out of austerity into a socially responsible, progressive country. Part of that work is a national, concerted effort to rethink its processes of engagement with those who are marginalized from decision-making. IT2 has become an important mechanism through which my professional credibility and integrity in contributing a small yet evidenced methodological approach to support that wider aim is further recognized.

Josephine Kwhali

When Dr Gabriel first asked me to contribute to IT1, I could not have imagined how powerful, painful and poignant the process would be. The sisters have provided insights, reflections and warmth, as we shared our stories, our hurts and our successes. I have been humbled by the wealth of experience that has been amassed, the wide range of initiatives we have undertaken and the significance of our collective presence in HE. We have been able to talk and laugh with each other without having to justify our experiences and without being confronted by faces reflecting disbelief, denial, guilt, embarrassment, indifference or anger. When energy has flagged I have been supported by the sisterhood and energized by the validity of the project and the response to it.

At times the process has been painful, that pain often borne alone. I have emotionally revisited the scripts on which my childhood memories have been crafted; an era when racist abuse was incessant and where it often appeared as if I had no right to exist. I have felt sadness in hearing the struggles of my sisters and reflected on the crushed dreams, the tenacity, courage and determination represented in each chapter of the book. I have felt anger that the expertise formed by experience does not seem to apply to Black people, and that our theoretical writings are often ignored. I have re-read literature that contributed to my intellectual and political growth when I was younger. I have discovered new material and have been reminded that each generation has much to learn from the others.

The project has re-invoked my sadness in knowing that Black people's contribution to social work education and the price paid by their invisibility have never been publicly acknowledged. I have felt weary as predominantly White academics have seemingly become experts on anti-racist social work, writing as if they discovered racism in the last few years. Some are critical of past efforts about which they knew little and contributed and suffered still less. I have been reminded that organizations and institutions will accept race initiatives that reflect positively on them or those that might succeed in silencing or marginalizing Black dissent. But if strategic change challenges dominant group interests it is attacked, crushed, reframed into more acceptable language or undermined by voices co-opted for that purpose. I think first about the need to build alliances across and outside academia, to care for each other and to be gentle on ourselves.

There is poignancy in knowing that I am one tiny speck in history, one Black woman in a chain of Black women stretching back across time, trying to claim the fullness of our own and each other's humanness. Black women, rich in our diversity, battered by waves of racism, sexism, class and other inequalities, yet unbowed and never still: 'Bringing the gifts that my ancestors gave / we are indeed the dream and the hope of the slave' (Maya Angelou, 1978).

REFERENCES
Angelou, M. (1978) *And Still I Rise*. New York: Random House.

Participatory witnessing: In conversation with my sisters

2

Decoloniality and intersectional feminism: In conversation with Shirley Anne Tate

Deborah Gabriel

Introduction

Shirley Anne Tate made history when she became the first Professor of Race and Education and founder of the Centre for Race, Education and Decoloniality in the Carnegie School of Education at Leeds Beckett University. It affirmed her pioneering work around decoloniality in research, education practice and institutional culture, of which Black feminism and intersectionality has been an integral component. She has published extensively around institutional racism, decoloniality, Black women's bodies, affect, performativity and beauty, and she is a Patron of Black British Academics. In 2019 she left the UK to take up her post as Canada Research Chair Tier 1 (designate) in Feminism and Intersectionality and Professor in the Sociology Department at the University of Alberta, Canada.

The conversation

Deborah

First, I just want to touch on your new role as Tier 1 Canada Chair in Feminism and Intersectionality at the University of Alberta. Can you tell me what the role entails, why you decided to leave the UK and what you hope to achieve in your new job in terms of social justice and equality?

Shirley

At the moment I'm Canada Tier 1 Research Chair Designate as I still have to go through a process of putting in an application to the Government of Canada to get funding for my research project. The research I am planning to do is a continuation of the social justice transformation work that I started in the UK and was involved with in South Africa. This research project is for the next seven years and would be funded by the Canadian government. I will be looking at the experiences of racism among Black and indigenous people and people of colour – that's faculty and students – in order to generate new approaches to curriculum development and institutional culture, which will facilitate the emergence of social justice transformation. This is across a variety of societies, not just Canada; societies that have experienced colonialism and still have indigenous populations and populations of Black people and people of colour that experience racism and are marginalized. I'll be looking at Canada, Sweden, Finland, Norway and South Africa. What I want to develop throughout the project is training for what they call here BIPOC (Black, Indigenous and People of Colour) students that will enable them to become researchers of institutional racism and anti-Black woman racism, because it's about intersectional, institutional racism. I want to enable more BIPOC academics to participate in academia, so I'm going to be training PhD students who will then become members of faculty.

Deborah
That's so admirable because that is part of the problem isn't it… the under-representation of Black academics and academics of colour?

Shirley
For me, the thing that really attracted me to Canada is that I will get funding to do the work that I want to do and have been doing for some time. In the UK, I think that the social justice transformation project has stalled, and it has been made to stall because of the intervention of the institution. Even the part of the project that has been taken on board, you know, the White curriculum project, even that has been sidelined, really. It's like, just put one Black woman here and one Black man there; that's not what I signed up for. This approach is about marginalizing what is increasingly seen as Black problems and people-of-colour problems, rather than a problem of the institution. I think social justice transformation in the UK just won't happen to the extent that it is needed, so we still have a Black student and student of colour attainment gap into the next century, most likely.

Deborah
Do you think the lack of people of colour in leadership roles limits the potential for radical change?

Shirley
Yes, I think that is a problem. It's a matter of numbers, but it's also a matter of White protectionism. They protect their culture because they get something

from it; they protect their curriculum because they get something from it, and they protect jobs for each other because they get something from it. We don't get promoted because they won't get anything from that, and they do not negotiate to keep us in the institution when we get a better offer elsewhere because they don't get anything from that. So, to say we need more Black people and people of colour is completely true. We work in institutions that are basically anti-Black. At the minute I'm writing something for a talk at a conference and it's related to the question: Why is it impossible to promote Black women? Why is it such an impossible thing to say okay, I'll give you another £10,000 to stay here because we don't want to lose you? Why is it such an impossible thing when we as Black women are still commodities in academia and contribute so much? For example, look at all the work you have done... it's about that work not being valued because we do not pander to Whiteness, we critique it and make it shake a little. We have had to learn how to work through the pain we experience or go somewhere else. It's either that or we collapse under the burden of it.

Deborah

That is why I feel it is so important that we have each other, protect each other and support each other.

Shirley

I think that is completely right. In my latter years in academia I have made the distinction between doing what is required within the institution and ensuring I do other things outside the university with my community, whether it is social activities or friendships. It is about what I need; the sustenance that you need to survive all these experiences we are faced with. As Jenny [Douglas] always says, our wellbeing is paramount and that is not just our physical wellbeing but our mental wellbeing. We should never underestimate what all the negativity that we experience does to us.

Deborah

For me, my coping mechanism for the trauma I experience in academia is theorizing my inequality to try to make sense of it. When I become analytical it empowers me. So I wanted to ask you, when you wrote your chapter for IT1, whether analysing and theorizing your experience helped you come to terms with what happened to you?

Shirley

Yes, definitely, because it helps me to understand how Whiteness works and therefore what I will need to do to challenge it and keep it at bay. That's the thing about Whiteness, it seeps into you in ways you don't even notice. One of the things that has been really important to me is that daily analysis of institutions that I have to perform in in order to remain in them. I don't think that I'm unusual in that; I think that Black people and people of colour in the UK have got to do that wherever they work. You have to understand daily racisms in order to understand that you are not the problem. It's not you, it is the institution; it's the person that looked at you in a really odd way or said something like 'Isn't there a strange smell in here today?' when you walk past them. It is the colleagues who see you walking down the corridor and turn their heads away rather than say hello, or you say hello and they ignore you. You are not the problem. If you do not have an analysis of the institution and how White supremacy works, then you begin to inhabit the space of the Black problem. The first time I spoke about this and brought it outside family and friendship circles was around 2010. I was speaking to a group of Black Brazilian researchers on the Black experience in higher education. I spoke for about twenty minutes as it was a panel discussion and I started with the figures on Black employment, then I spoke about lived experience. When I finished the whole room was completely stunned, and whether they were from Brazil or the US they said they had exactly the same experiences. That made me realize the importance of giving voice to all of this, and that is why IT1 was so important. When we did the first book launch in London it was so important for Black women to hear that because often we cannot say it. White people accuse us of being racist towards them when we speak the truth because they don't understand what racism really means. In the present context anybody can be racist towards anybody; that's what they think because they do not know what racism means. So yes, it is important to have continuous analysis, especially because things are constantly changing. Sometimes White people think they have a really good relationship with you that entitles them to say really awful things and think that you will sit there and take it... it doesn't matter, it's just you, I know you, you're my friend. But it does matter; you're not my friend if you say things like that.

Deborah
Can you give me an example?

Shirley
I'll give you an example. It didn't have to do with Black people or with me specifically. I was in a meeting and I didn't know the person who said it that well but afterwards I was talking to someone else whom I have worked with for many years and she repeated it. The comment was anti-Chinese. The

person said that Chinese international students are spoiling the educational experience for other students in the class. I said in the meeting that these Chinese students are financing the entire higher education system in the UK and they deserve a good education. When we left, the colleague I work with said, 'But it's really true… you end up with a classroom just full of Chinese students, what do you do with that?' Because I'm not Chinese she thought it was okay to say that to me, but no, it wasn't because that was racist and I had to call it out. I'm increasingly becoming very wary of people that do critical Whiteness studies and proclaim themselves to be White anti-racists, especially when their actions continue to perpetrate the very racism that they claim to speak against.

Deborah

To me it's an appropriation of critical race theory. Too often there is a failure on their part to acknowledge their White privilege and how they benefit materially from their Whiteness.

Shirley

Nothing changes because they continue to engage in the pervasive White friendships and White networks that they benefit from in terms of promotion and their appropriation of Black theories. When it comes to ordinary interactions with Black people you see the racism staring you in the face. So I'm beginning to be very sceptical of anti-racist White people, especially those who, as you say, do not recognize their own privilege and don't recognize the daily exclusions that they participate in within institutions.

Deborah

That brings me to the next area of discussion, which is that you have undertaken a lot of transformational work around decoloniality. It's a term that has become fashionable and has been institutionally appropriated; so I want to ask, what is your definition of decoloniality?

Shirley

I take my definition of decoloniality from Caribbean thinkers like Fanon (1986) and Césaire (2004). Their work is also being used, especially Fanon, by Latin American thinkers of colour, so I take my definition from there. One of the things that struck me about Fanon when I read the book is what he says about the struggle to become a Black man. It's about looking at how colonialism and colonial constructions still impact us today on the level of knowledge about us as Black people and people of colour and on the level of how White supremacy still operates on a colonial basis in which the only human is White. Decoloniality is also concerned with how different knowledge systems always have a persistent thread that is about Black inferiority, White superiority and how that continues to be perpetuated even today. It is about how it affects us now, and a lot of it is to do with feelings of superiority that White people have and feelings of inferiority that are imprinted on Black people. These have colonial origins and enslavement/indentureship origins and it's about thinking 'what are we going to do to counter that?' To me that is decolonization, which is an active process. It is not just using the word, it is about diminishing White supremacy that we still live with in the Western hemisphere. I understand your discomfort because I still feel discomfort about the way the term decolonization is being used, especially by White academics in the UK who have no investment in making that happen. It has just become another buzzword and I really resent that because it is a necessary part of the transformational change that we need to make in society. It is uncomfortable for me because there are people using it who have no interest in changing it and who just quote Black scholars' work but don't look at race and racism. You never see White supremacy as a problem when you're doing decolonial work as a White person. You never think, oh, that means I have to change this whole canon that I have been inculcated in from the time I started doing sociology; you never think you have to do that. No, you can just keep using it as a theory. But with decolonization change has to happen. Decoloniality has just become a concept rather than a process.

Deborah

I find I need to constantly keep decolonizing my own mind to be my authentic self... it is something we have to do on a personal level as colonized people of colour, which is not something that White people have to do.

Shirley

One of the goals I set myself many years ago is to build pipelines, so we cannot just be here, we have to have other people coming behind us to fill our places when we leave, because we will leave... we will either die or retire or be made redundant. That is a task we have as older academics; to make sure that there are other people there to keep the anti-racist decolonial project going. Otherwise, all our work will come to nothing.

Deborah

You have hit the nail on the head. I started to realize that over the last couple of years, which is why I have gone out of my way to cultivate meaningful

relationships with students of colour. I came to this realization that there is
no sense of priority in increasing the number of Black academics but there
is an urgent need for positive action. Proportionally more students of colour
attend university but do not end up in academia.

Shirley

That's a problem we have, and one of the things I realized is the reason they
don't end up in academia is because they are never mentored to do that. I
used to have Black students and students of colour and I used to ask them if
anyone had spoken to them about doing a masters or PhD and they would
always say I was the first person to mention it to them. If you look at MA
courses, you don't see many Black people or people of colour on them and
there is no reason why they should not be there.

Deborah

These are the kinds of changes that we need to see, so I can see the attraction
in moving to Canada where the government invests money in research that
is going to facilitate change and give you the opportunity to train Black,
indigenous and people of colour in these academic roles.

I want to talk about your work on Black feminism and intersectionality
and how you manage to embed that into your work on decoloniality. Often,
they are treated as separate issues, but surely the anti-Black racism we
have seen directed towards women of colour suggests they are part of the
same thing?

Shirley

One of the issues over the way that decoloniality has been adopted, especially
by White scholars in the UK, is that they forget anti-racism is a significant
part of the decolonization project. You cannot separate racism from
decolonization as it is an integral part of the colonial project... racism is
incredibly intersectional, and we know from the experiences of Black women
that it can be quite different from the experiences of Black men, and that
straight women have different experiences from lesbians. For me, it is really
important to avoid this homogenization that you sometimes get when men
do theory. Charles Mills did a talk at Leeds once and it was a fantastic talk
and the room was full. He was talking about the social contract in which
White men achieve superiority, so they get the most from this social contract.
Then White women and non-White men are the next group of people to get
something from it. Then the people who can never be signatories to that
contract are Black women. So you see, to not think in an intersectional way

when you think about racism or decolonization is missing a big part of the picture. For me, the decolonial project is about decoloniality and it is about racism, sexism, patriarchy and homophobia.

Deborah
What do you think is our most effective strategy as women of colour in academia? Do you think the focus should be on changing the system or that resistance and change come from within ourselves?

Shirley
I think that's a really good question, Deborah, and I think they are connected. I was very lucky to have been born and brought up in Jamaica up to the age of 20. It gave me a particular perspective on what it means to be a Black person of African descent and also what it means in terms of what a society could look like. While Jamaica is a very unequal society, there are Black doctors, Black nurses, Black teachers, a Black Prime Minister… so for me that was never an impossibility. To then come to the UK and see my people faced with a situation where that was never a possibility was a very hard thing for me in 1975. It made me want to teach – I was a teacher to begin with. I never taught in a school but that is what I did because I thought it was really important to change the way we see ourselves in order to effect change. Bob Marley says it: that we must emancipate ourselves from slavery, and Frantz Fanon says it in the colonial psyche. So we know that is a big part of what we need to do in the decolonial project. We need to change our psyche and our minds, at the same time as trying to change higher education institutions through our work. One of the things that has always been important to me as an academic is to remember who I am. Sometimes you can get caught up in academia and thinking everybody's reading my work… I've been invited here, I've been invited there… people will listen to what I'm saying. You can get big-headed and forget that you are one person, so for me humility is always important. We can't afford to get swept along with this wave of I am this and I am that. That is also the way racism works… it works to make us feel special, like we are unique. But special and unique can be chopped off at the knees so it is important to stay connected. I cannot do it by myself and there is no way I should even think that. It has to be something a community does… that is what Black feminism teaches us. Everybody has to be involved in this project because the project is bigger than you and you cannot think you can do it by yourself, as that is delusional.

Deborah

What advice would you give to young Black women who might be graduates who like doing research and are wondering whether there is a place for them in academia? Given the low numbers of Black women in the academy you could understand why they may feel they do not belong there.

Shirley

I would have to say: Get a Black mentor you can trust. I never had a mentor but certainly two people kept me in education earlier on when I was doing my undergraduate degree. They weren't from my community group but they were people of colour. Black people have a political project, which is that we must enable other Black people to get up. They kept me in education after I was there for one term and was going to leave. They said, stay, it gets easier. I would suggest that they get a mentor they can trust. Even if they have to send emails to people and phone people, most Black women I know would be very pleased to give advice to other Black women who are thinking of entering academia in terms of a career. The second thing they should do... what has helped me to survive all the trauma, is to not just be an academic. To know that my community exists outside the university and being an academic is not the only thing in my life. I don't have to talk about the latest book I've read... I can talk about other things, like what I cooked for dinner last night, with people outside that context like family members and other community people and people I have volunteered with for many years. They fed the parts of me that being a Black academic cannot feed. Don't fall into the trap of always having to account for yourself... 'what are you working on now then?' That is not important. What is important is how do you feel at the moment? Are you alright? Would you like something to eat? That's more important. I think in terms of thinking about yourself as a whole person, not just one aspect.

Deborah

If you had to pick one piece of research that is your favourite, what would it be?

Shirley

I would have to choose my Black Women's Bodies book because that comes out of my beauty project that is still ongoing. I liked writing that book... I enjoyed it very much. Then, on the institutional racism side, the first ever journal article that got published for me was an amazing feat because I went through a lot to write it. Once I started writing it after years of analysis it just came out because I found a way to write about it that was very personal but also impersonal at the same time! So that one, because it freed me to write about other aspects of institutional racism and its effect on economies, which I hadn't known how to do before. I owe an enormous debt to Black feminist theory and critical race theory for allowing me to think about autoethnography as a way to write, especially within my discipline, sociology. [Without that] I could never have done it.

Deborah

Do you think one way we are held back in academia is based around what kind of research is valued and how it is rewarded? I found myself defending my research on my unsuccessful promotion panel interview where a male academic of colour commented: 'your research... race this, race that... but what is your research profile?' I could not have made it clearer that my research is centred on social justice and critical race pedagogy, media, culture social and political communication and draws heavily on Black feminism and critical race theory. I was told I had not produced enough journal articles and responded that my most impactful research was undertaken through books and book chapters.

Shirley

I think Black feminist theory, Black decolonial feminist theory, research on Blackness and research on racism are just not valued within institutions, just like we are not valued. I had a similar experience after the last REF [Research Excellence Framework]. We immediately had a draft review and I submitted about seven items, a combination of journal articles and book chapters. Do you know what the director of research, a White woman, said to me? What is this journal on ethnic and racial studies?, I've never heard of it. I replied that it's one of the best journals in the country. She said to me: you have been publishing, but Shirley it's quality not quantity that counts. The point is that they cannot judge our research as they don't understand it. It is about trying to demonstrate our lack of value within our institutions. But we cannot let it get to us. There is something important about giving back and this has always been an important part of Black community development. When I was growing up in Jamaica it was instilled in me as a young child that we have to give back to our community in whatever way. When I was 14 I did volunteer work with the National Literacy Programme and on Live Labour Day people clean the churchyard and things like that, as that was a way of giving back. I think we have to see it as part of our political project as we must always have an eye to the future. One of the things that racism tries to do is to rob us of thinking about our future prospects or what the political project might look like in ten years. I discovered that through the anguish I experienced on a daily basis... I thought about the anguish all the time and became drawn into it, rather than doing things that might help others or myself. So we cannot let racism make us think only of the present.

Deborah

Shirley, thank you so much for sharing your personal experiences and critical analysis with me.

REFERENCES

Césaire, A. (2004) *Discours sur le colonialisme suivi de Discours sur la Négritude.*
   Paris: Présence Africaine [originally published 1950 and 1987 respectively].
Fanon, F. (1986) *Black Skin, White Masks.* London: Pluto Classics.

Theoretical insights

Shirley's frank discussion with me on Whiteness in the academy serves as a reminder of the ongoing importance of the decolonial project and the need to recognize the ways in which people of colour are impacted by Whiteness. Crucially, for decolonization to be effective, decoloniality must be defined in accordance with its earliest proponents: the colonized peoples of African, Caribbean and Latin American descent and indigenous peoples who recognized the importance of freeing themselves from mental slavery and its destructive imprint. The route to emancipation and liberation from colonization is subjectivity and its facilitation of critical and theoretical analysis that yields clarity and understanding about the manifestations of racial oppression and White supremacy. Of major significance is Shirley's assertion that intersectional gender equality is a prerequisite to decoloniality, given the multiple levels and layers of racial inequality shaped by gender. Slavery, colonialism and neo-colonialism must be acknowledged as patriarchal, sexist and misogynistic projects in which Black women have historically been dehumanized, objectified and devalued. hooks (1994: 63) touches on this in her discussion of the persistence of routine undermining of women of colour's status in the academy. She argues there is an unhealthy 'alliance' between White men and women whose dominance and imposition of academic standards determine what is of intellectual value and what is not, which leads to the devaluing of our work as Black women and women of colour, either deeming it as not theoretical enough or as too deviant from their imposed norms. I believe a key component of the decolonial project is a close examination of the alliance to which hooks refers, and how it facilitates social closure (Gabriel, 2018). The other important area of Shirley's work is highlighting the need to remain grounded as academics in our communities, to nurture relationships with families and friends and to give back to our communities in a variety of ways beyond academia. This is a key aspect of the decolonial project; in recognizing that we can and ought to contribute to community development independent of the research that we do in which people of colour are subjects of that research. As Shirley asserts, immersing ourselves in our communities helps us to be externally focused and to be thinking beyond our status as victims, to be empowered individuals with hopes and dreams for a future of numerous possibilities.

REFERENCES

Gabriel, D. (2018) 'Social closure, White male privilege and female complicity: Why gender equality still has a long way to go'. Online. www.academia. edu/37661796/Social_closure_White_male_privilege_and_female_complicity_ why_gender_equality_still_has_a_long_way_to_go (accessed 12 January 2020).

hooks, b. (1994) *Teaching to Transgress: Education as the practice of freedom.* London: Routledge.

Chapter 8

Disrupting Whiteness in higher education through Teaching Within: In conversation with Aisha Richards

Deborah Gabriel

Introduction

Shades of Noir's Teaching Within programme is an academic progression intervention that responds directly to the under-representation of academics of colour in the creative arts and design higher education sector. It was created in 2016 by Aisha Richards and has been delivered across all six colleges of University of the Arts London (UAL), increasing academic representation of creatives of colour by 20 per cent in the past three years. Teaching Within is also a response to the Teaching and Research Careers Pipeline, a key strand of the Race Champions Forum Project for aspiring academic graduates and staff not in academic roles, with degrees in related subjects. The programme aims to support a full cycle of development, value cultural currency and create opportunities for people of colour. In addition to developing Teaching Within, Aisha also contributed to the creation, development and delivery of the postgraduate teaching qualification module entitled Inclusive Teaching and Learning, and was awarded UAL's first Teaching Award in 2017, nominated by students.

The conversation
Deborah

As a preliminary to talking about Teaching Within, my first point is the obvious observation that there are so few women of colour in academia as lecturers and that's despite the growth we've seen in the numbers of students of colour. What impact do you think it has on students of colour not to have us teaching them?

Aisha

I think it has a huge impact. The first part of it is the role model aspect... as soon as you see someone that looks like you in an academic role you wonder about them – in fact they ask me directly how I got into academia. I remember when I did my research 'Any Room at the Inn?' in 2009 and spoke to recent graduates of colour and they were all so shocked that I was an academic. When you see people of colour in higher education there's an assumption that you're not an academic, but when students find out they do talk quite purposefully about the importance of seeing us, the pain they suffer at not seeing us and the effect it has on their experience and sense of belonging in academia.

Deborah

Do you think there being so few women of colour academics can have an adverse effect? That because the senior staff are predominantly White they see them as the authority, the authentic academics and us as lesser? Sometimes I've had students of colour who have really engaged, and you can see they're happy and smiling and proud that you're there with this knowledge and expertise on issues that affect them. But sometimes I think students of colour doubt our expertise.

Aisha

I absolutely agree with that. I would go a step further and say that sometimes because we've been trained to think a certain way, even when the curriculum is centred around social justice they still feel it's not right.

Deborah

So you see how we're caught, how the Eurocentric curriculum and lack of diversity can adversely affect their thinking? The other point I wanted to make was, based on your experience, how does Whiteness create barriers to the recruitment of women of colour as lecturers? It doesn't seem to me to be a lack of motivation, as often when I do talk to students and graduates there is interest in becoming academics.

Aisha

I think there are two key areas. The first is mainstream recruitment practice, the selection and shortlisting before it even gets to the panel. If it's an HR algorithm, there's been all sorts of data which show that the algorithms are predominantly created by White men. So there are technical, systemic barriers around Whiteness and bias that are replicated in the technologies that are supposed to be neutral and objective. The second part is that even when we are given a platform to teach and become part of an academic community, there is inequality in how our peers, who are predominantly White, engage with us. It's about how people talk to you, what they expect from you. In my view if they have low expectations of us as their peers as academics of colour, it doesn't surprise me that there are such low expectations of students of colour. People of colour generally know they have to work harder as most of us are told that from a very young age. So most of the time these are exceptional individuals and then there is a resistance around that. How is it that so many Black female academics that I know are exceptional, yet so few of them are professors? It doesn't make any sense other than there is a very strong bias, structural and institutional racism, that exists among those with the decision-making power in recruitment.

Deborah

I guess it's about privilege ... those with the power to determine who is deemed worthy of certain academic positions and how our knowledge, skills and expertise are judged and, more often, not valued. Those who assimilate are more likely to be judged favourably, and those who challenge the status quo judged harshly. This is a longstanding issue. Clearly there are currently no effective measures to substantially increase the number of Black academics, despite the impact on students of colour's sense of belonging. There is no sense of priority within the institutions, so the solutions must come from us as we see the barriers that hold us back, right?

Aisha

I think the first thing here is the issue of trust... who has earned it and who has not. Given the history of the lack of representation, the trust in the institution around this area among both existing members of staff and those considering an academic career. There are also students who are not of colour who are saying this is wrong and makes no sense unless there is something untoward taking place. That was the first thing I relayed to my institution... my lack of trust in them.

Deborah

You mean lack of trust in their ability to effect change?

Aisha

Yes. It comes from a place of seeing that they don't understand themselves and how their practices impact us. I spoke to them at great length about the issue of trust and the trust that Shades of Noir built, which had to be earned. Not enough is being done to make us feel safe that we can apply for a job and get what we deserve fairly. It was very important for the institution to understand that they have not built that trust. I would say that no institution in the UK has yet built that trust, judging by the initiatives that have taken place across the UK and the models of practice that seem tokenistic. There isn't really a community of practitioners. I'm referring to mentor-type schemes and the practice of adding a few lines to job adverts saying they welcome diversity. With Shades of Noir, mutual benefit lies at the heart of what we do, so if we are taking something from someone or a group of people we try to give something back. For example, if we have speakers that contribute to our programme, we try to have a year-long relationship as a minimum and encourage those individuals to be part of other activities. Thinking about Teaching Within – that feeds into our practice. So those individuals who have already contributed and demonstrated a commitment to social justice are the types of individuals we would consider to be perfect for an academic career and inspiring our student population irrespective of their race. For us it's important for students to know they have somebody who cares. I don't think we talk about the caring part in teaching; we don't talk about how, in teaching, we are the guardians of these individuals and within that guardianship, there should be a level of care and responsibility for each and every student, in my opinion. What we have tried to do with the programme is to utilize these individuals that have given to the sector, the institution or directly to Shades of Noir and follow it up with an opportunity. It's not an open recruitment process – in fact it's quite closed. We've done that because we don't want to interview people. We share opportunities with the individuals and communities that we have already engaged with and give them the option of being part of the programme. We don't advertise Teaching Within on our website as we have found that when individuals complete our programme they have been approached by various parts of the institution who want to enlist them to undertake tokenistic work.

Deborah

You mean they're using the intellectual capital of the Teaching Within programme to make themselves look progressive on issues of diversity, rather than changing their structures, systems, processes and practices?

Aisha

Yes – and their behaviours. An institution is a big place with frameworks, policies and procedures but they are all impacted by the individuals that work there. Many of these individuals don't understand what it means to be an anti-racist advocate and what it looks like to behave in a mutually beneficial way. It's taken some time for us to work with the institution for them to develop understanding around this.

Deborah

Do you think that diversity as a concept has been appropriated within the corporate, marketized environment in academia, and is essentially depoliticized and disconnected from social justice?

Aisha

Yes, absolutely. The misappropriation of our work happens often. Shades of Noir and all our work is steeped in and comes from pain and that cannot be replicated, nor the life experience that has caused the pain. As a Black woman born and educated in the UK, I have navigated racist structures throughout my life and the nuances of what that means to me personally. I have all sorts of thoughts and ideas on how things can change but I don't believe that an institution predominantly run by White folk has the knowledge and life experience to deliver this work in the way I do.

Deborah

How do you deal with attempts to appropriate Shades of Noir's work and the hijacking of its social justice agenda?

Aisha

I'm in a privileged position in that Shades of Noir is not owned by the institution. This is the first time I have openly shared information about the programme. The university does not have the right to talk about the programme, even though I know they really want to, because it is a success. We've had 40 individuals complete the programme and over 80 per cent are people of colour. Out of those 40 people, 29 now have teaching roles. There is one case I am especially proud of. One of the individuals who completed the programme previously worked in an administrative role within our institution and they now have a part-time post at one of the most prestigious colleges within our institution. They have not only changed their career path; their life has changed. They told me their financial position has greatly improved and subsequently their children's lives have changed for the better.

Deborah

What are the specific factors in the Teaching Within programme that lead to that kind of change?

Aisha

I think the core part of the programme builds trust and self-belief. Right at the start I tell the participants they are all awesome and that the institution is very lucky to have them. Through the Teaching Within programme, participants complete their postgraduate teaching certificate in academic practice and the Shades of Noir team are with them throughout the programme, offering additional support. They have a whole community they can call on and undertake tasks collaboratively, such as research but also social activities as well.

Deborah

How would you describe the Teaching Within programme in a sentence?

Aisha

I've got a quote, rather than a sentence. It's by Margaret Mead and I use it often: 'It only takes a few thoughtful citizens to change the world.' In my mind, the Teaching Within participants are those thoughtful citizens and the programme brings these thoughtful citizens together to transform the institution.

Deborah

That's a wonderful thought. Building on that transformation in education practice, how does the Teaching Within programme enhance the learning experience for students of colour?

Aisha

The Teaching Within programme disrupts the Whiteness of the institution as social justice practitioners and helps to decolonize the curriculum and creative arts practice. The participants are from very diverse backgrounds. Over 50 per cent have a disability and 15 per cent are from the LGBTQ community, so the Teaching Within programme is unique in offering intersectional perspectives, which feed through into the mainstream teaching environment. Everyone on the Teaching Within programme has direct access to deans and associate deans, so it's not just about including Black and Brown people, it's about including people of colour who are empowered and whose voices are heard.

Deborah

What advice would you give to women of colour working in isolation in higher education institutions who feel powerless?

Aisha

I would say: find people you can talk to. Over the years things have changed for me at the institutions I work in, but for a very long time I was on my own and it was a very lonely place. So my advice is to seek people out, even if they are in different roles to you. There are many people of colour who work in the library or in administrative or operational roles who have Masters qualifications, MBAs and PhDs, are school governors or run their own business. They have been my saving grace. They made me realize I wasn't alone and that the problems I experienced were shared by others. Their knowledge and experience have helped me immensely.

Deborah

Teaching Within is a perfect example of how it is sometimes necessary to go outside the existing framework to bring about radical change, given that the programme is not owned by the institution.

Aisha

We have no choice but to work outside the frameworks of the institution if we want meaningful change. It's trial and error but if we don't try then there is no possibility for change.

Deborah

I'm glad you said that because the 'models' referred to in the title of this volume are not in the Eurocentric sense of a bureaucratic template that can be followed to the letter and produce a uniform outcome.

Aisha

The other day someone asked me to share the 'blueprint' for Shades of Noir so that others can succeed in this way. My response was that I cannot say with any certainty that if I were someone else and my team members were different that we would have the same outcomes.

Deborah

I think that it's because we are so unique and work in a more liberal way that we are not valued within our institutions... because we do not conform to the prescribed notions of education in what has become a very autocratic environment in higher education. Thank you so much for your valuable insights.

Deborah Gabriel

Theoretical insights

Aisha's work through Shades of Noir is hugely transformational in the way that it is focused on tackling two key areas of inequity in academia: the under-representation (which should really be conceptualized as the exclusion of certain groups of people of colour from the academy, especially Black Caribbean, Bangladeshi, Pakistani and Black African peoples); and the Eurocentric curriculum, which is also exclusionary. Whiteness not only de-centres other cultures, but it also has the power to exclude by advancing White identity as the normative identity of an academic, which becomes the preferred identity in recruitment and progression. Aisha's Teaching Within programme is revolutionary in challenging the assumption that only certain qualifications, skills and knowledge are valuable for teaching in higher education. Her successful programme has demonstrated that given the opportunity, aspiring graduates and staff in administrative roles can not only be developed as lecturers in higher education, but they can also transform the experience of students of colour through their inclusive teaching practice, focused on social justice. A large part of the programme's effectiveness must be attributed to the cultivation of a supportive learning community that Aisha and her team nurture on an ongoing basis, and the way that it crosses boundaries and borders in bringing together a community of prospective educators from different ethnic and cultural backgrounds, in a way that actualizes intersectionality. This puts me in mind of hooks's argument about the need to build teaching communities that cross borders and boundaries:

> It is crucial that critical thinkers who want to change our teaching practices talk to one another, collaborate in a discussion that crosses boundaries and creates a space for intervention... often we have no concrete examples of individuals who actually occupy different locations within structures, sharing ideas with one another, mapping out terrains of commonality, connection, and shared concern with teaching practices. (hooks, 1994: 130)

References
hooks, b. (1994) *Teaching to Transgress: Education as the practice of freedom.* London: Routledge.

Chapter 9

The power of story: Leading conversations of inclusion, equity and justice through community engagement: In conversation with Virginia Cumberbatch
Deborah Gabriel

Introduction
Virginia Cumberbatch is director of the Community Engagement Center at the University of Texas (UT) at Austin. Her role includes incubating the Social Justice Institute and connecting the resources of the university to the community to address concerns of equity and access in education, housing and healthcare. Under her leadership, Virginia has cast a new vision for the centre, positioning it as the front porch of the university, a space of trust, reciprocity, reconciliation, and mutually beneficial partnerships to serve historically underserved communities of colour. In 2015 she co-founded Hux Storyhouse, a creative strategies collective that uses culturally relevant storytelling to help organizations and institutions engage thoughtfully and authentically with markets across the Black Diaspora.

The conversation
Deborah
Virginia, can I ask your age please, because you are the youngest contributor to IT2 and I think it's important for our readers to know how much you have achieved already in your lifetime at a relatively young age (compared to the rest of us)!

Virginia
[Laughs.] You should never ask a lady her age! I'm 31.

Deborah

When we met at the diversity conference in Austin in 2018, I was admiring of your work around community engagement and equity. As our friendship blossomed, we later discovered similarities in our work centred on Black women's health and wellbeing. I'd like to touch on those during our discussion, but first I'd like to talk about your work around community engagement. Tell me, how does Black feminism inform your work?

Virginia

It's interesting, because feminism in terms of the strict definition of it, and what we in the US have come to perceive as feminism, does not align with my own personal ethos. As I have grown older and matured, I have realized I had been exposed to a very linear understanding of feminism. It was this idea of women power and the sense that it was around sexuality and reclaiming that. I think this demonstrates that I was exposed to the appropriation of feminism by White women. Once I had an understanding of the incredible legacy and precedent that has been set by Black women to approach feminism from an intersectional perspective that includes racial justice, I came to admire the political and social critique of women who identify as Black feminists.

From the Toni Morrisons of the world to the Angela Davises of the world, you realize there is no demarcation between those identities. This creates a more thoughtful approach to how we dismantle systems of oppression. When I think of it that way, there are so many principles that have been associated with Black feminism that are inherent in the work that I do. For example, we cannot talk about housing without talking about health, and we cannot talk about health without talking about education. More importantly, we cannot talk about any of these things until we are willing to truly reconcile and sit with the consequences of institutionalized racism and how that is the foundation of all these systems. To me, that is the main ethos of Black feminism: challenging systems comprehensively and thoughtfully, about all these intersectional identities and how throughout the Western world we have oppressed people.

The other key thing I have pulled from Black feminism is that there is such a beautiful resilience as well as hope in the work that Black women drive. Listening to you do your radio interview this week (Black British Academics, 2019) ... yes it is hard work that we do, it is our lived experience but in it we always find the hope, the beauty, the resilience in being a community of people – it's part of our inherent legacy as Black women. That is something I try to maintain in the work that I do: to create spaces for rest and boundaries for what we are willing to engage in, so we don't have burnout and we do not continue to expose ourselves to trauma. Also, just the pure joy of working alongside other Black women and women of colour in doing this work.

Deborah
One thing I have come to appreciate being here in Austin, especially when you took me on the tour of Clarksville to see the history of Black people's experiences here, is how much your work is connected to that past and aims to address those injustices. In your view, what are some of the ways that Black women continue to be impacted by those legacies of historical racial injustice?

Virginia
Austin serves as a microcosm of the larger systems and narratives of America in that it is too easy to accept the convenient narrative that Austin is a thriving city and fun place to live, with good food and a technology centre. This is a similar narrative to the US as a whole. We are the most powerful nation in the world and people can come here and find the American Dream. But then there is this inconvenient narrative that is foundational to who we are as a city and a country, which is that we have never truly had the reckoning of the way in which this city, and the power and vitality of the city, is based on creating spaces for the haves and have nots.

Systemic decisions and policies that develop a clear separation between who gets access to education and who does not; who gets access to economic development and who does not; who gets access to quality housing and who does not. This is replicated across America as a whole. Until we have a reckoning, a repentance and a reversal of systems that benefited from slavery, the annihilation of indigenous people, the inequity of Latinx communities, and the nurturing of environments and systems that perpetuate colonial, capitalistic greed, we will continue to see communities of colour not only strive to navigate these systems but also become victims of these systems.

What I see in Austin around the experience of Black women is a numbers game in many ways and I know this is resonant with Black women in the UK when we talk about Black women navigating the academic environment. The issue in Austin is yes, we want to see more of us as there is power in numbers, not just because of the visibility it brings but because of the collectiveness it creates in not feeling like you are waging this war alone.

What has happened in Austin is that a lot of Black women have been burned out and worn out as we have been waging this war alone – or it feels that way – and in many cases trying to infiltrate spaces that traditionally have not been open to us. For example, sitting on boards that have never seen a young Black woman. I would love to do a research project to see if I am the only Black woman under 40 to sit on these boards. It is so exhausting to always be the only one at the table where people are turning to you and you have to call people out... it's exhausting! I did that in graduate school, I have done it in every job I have had and every board I have sat on. So, we have to create our own tables.

In the past few years we have seen new organizations being developed and run by Black women whose attitude is that they are just going to develop what is needed and not rely on the system. A prime example is Mimi Styles who founded an organization called Measure Austin that is based on her continued exasperation with the lack of transparency in our police system. There was no data and the city's response was that it had insufficient resources to collect data on how many Black people were being pulled over in comparison to White people. So Mimi said fine, I will build an organization to do this. Five years on, her organization has contracts to do that – to hold the city accountable.

We recognize we are operating in a privileged space, those of us who have access and sit on boards and have resources to start organizations. For the Black women who do not have these opportunities there is just as much trauma in those spaces. For example, having to be pulled away from your cultural hub because you can no longer afford to live in your community; or the health outcomes of living in a food desert; or the health outcomes that come with being unable to provide for your children in a certain way; or working overtime and not eating well – all of those things. These experiences are not unique to Austin, but they definitely have an impact on the cultural landscape of the city. If we have Black women who are suffering and stressing in silence and invisibility, it means there is less of their thought leadership and less of their cultural contribution and less of their melanin magic contributing in other areas of our city.

Deborah

These women are not just invisible to the mainstream but they're also invisible to academics like us because we're so over-burdened and focused on academia that we don't get enough time to spend with our communities. I guess your role as head of the Center for Community Engagement gives you an opportunity to have eyes and ears to know what's going on in the community.

Virginia

It is so critical for me as my reason for taking this job and sole purpose is to build access and engagement in the community. It just so happens that I get to do that with the resources of a top-tier institution. Those resources are fiscal, they are thought leadership, they are research and sometimes they are students. It's about prying open the doors of the university and saying there is a world outside this campus, and you are obligated to be a part of that community and to bring to fruition equity, opportunity and access. We pay for these things and part of this role is recognizing UT's complicity in inequity. What good is research if it just sits in isolation in a publication that ten academics read in a year? What good is research if it isn't rooted in the community voice? The community is saying these are the issues we are facing, this is what we would like to see happen in our community; how will your research impact that bottom line, how will it help us? Working alongside the community is of paramount importance; I use the term co-labour. I want to be a co-labourer.

As a university we should not be bulldozing our way into communities saying we have the answers. We should be working alongside the community simply to amplify and elevate their voice. So often research is conducted in isolation. We don't know the right questions to ask and we don't know the correct approach to take. We probably should not be asking someone to come to the campus to fill out a survey; we should be willing to go into their living rooms and have an understanding about their culture, their family, and engage in conversation with them. That is just as valuable as having some statistical survey done. I really encourage that type of academic scholarship, that activist scholarship which says I am conducting this research from the perspective of community engagement and community equity. That should be the prevailing value within my research so that we are not just asking the right questions but helping to illuminate some of the invisibility of these folks. I know when I had the pleasure of being in the UK with you and we were talking about the disparities in health outcomes, that up-to-date data was not available on how cancer is affecting Black women, or how obesity affects young Black boys. If we don't have those numbers we do not know how best to support the community. That invisibility is a scary place because invisibility is not just about not being seen. We value what we see so if the city does not see Black people, if they don't see Black women, they won't give priority to allocating resources to those people.

Deborah

Can you give me an example of a project that you've done based on those principles of co-labouring and giving the community a voice?

Virginia

We have a programme we run called the Front Porch Gathering. That is the metaphor we have been using for the past few years. We want to be the front porch of the university. In Texas, that's a really big deal because front porches are places of convening, places of safety and places of connection, and we want to be that to the community. We have approached this programme to be a recalibration of community engagement that is not us talking at the community in a town hall setting but is about us creating the time and space for the community to explore the priorities, to be a part of solution-making and to elevate their lived experience alongside stakeholders who are bringing data and insight.

Two or three years ago we did a research project called Those Who Have Stayed. It was around cultural erasure in the age of gentrification. That research was led by Dr Eric Tang (Tang and Ren, 2014) who explored why Black people are leaving Austin at unprecedented rates. He argued that all the focus on the people leaving ignored those who were staying and becoming culturally displaced. Leading the research, he invited two of his classes to examine that [issue] and they did a whole ethnography focused on central East Austin to learn the history of how East Austin was developed. Instead of doing surveys they identified people in each of the zip codes, knocked on doors, sat in their living rooms and asked them about their experience. Some of the perceptions that emerged from the community were: 'I feel like my new White neighbour cares more about their dogs than they do about me' or 'I feel like there are more dogs in this neighbourhood now than there are children'. Even if these perceptions are based on feelings and not statistics, they mean something.

We had one woman who came and brought a letter with her from a developer. Throughout the community people are getting unprecedented requests from developers to buy their homes so they can knock them down and build bigger houses. She lived in her home for sixty years, raised her children there and she had a letter that said it was time for her to move out and move on – and it had a pre-signed cheque attached to it. You can only imagine the psychological trauma of someone saying that your time in this community is up, without the slightest acknowledgement of what you have contributed to it.

We took that qualitative data and recognized that our role lies in facilitating these types of conversations. We have an opportunity to be part of the work around disruption, and last year we launched something called the Community Housing Hub. The aim is to be a conversational space around housing equity and affordable housing access. In doing the work we did through the Front Porch, we realized the issue is not just economic or about policy but that it has to be comprehensive. So, our approach to the community through the Community Housing Hub is focused on research, advocacy, and preservation of the history and culture that made this community. That is an example of being thoughtful and strategic about how to do community engagement and the benefits that come from it. We derived a lot of knowledge and understanding about the community that we would otherwise not have gained. Our research approach was about valuing lived experience, story and history as much as the economic aspects.

Deborah
What legacy would you like to leave for future generations?

Virginia
I would love to disrupt institutionalized racism in education. I would love to build housing equity in Austin. But in terms of the purpose I feel I have been called to do, it is helping people of colour to realize how valuable their stories are. Also, that their stories are not just for preservation, not just to talk about the pain and hurt of living in this country, but their stories are a powerful tool for disrupting all the injustices we have faced as a people.

Deborah
Do you think also that the stories are so powerful because of what we learn from them? That they are also educational?

Virginia
Exactly. When I think about the book I had the privilege of participating in (Vincent *et al.*, 2018), that book was not about saying we should just document this history. It was a healing process for people who were never seen, never heard, never valued – it was a healing process for them to be able to tell their own stories that were solidified in a book. The book is not only educational but a tool for the university to come to terms with things they had not fixed. The book was used in a recent case around hate speech and was used to support the decision to remove confederate statues from the campus. The book has also been used to galvanize current students of colour to be inspired by those in whose footsteps they tread – those who came before them – so that they are motivated for the work that still needs to be done. So yes, our stories are powerful and educational, as they are lessons learned and accounts of resilience. Telling your own story is the most healing experience a human being can have. Knowing that your story has left a footprint on this earth is really powerful.

Deborah
I totally agree. Thank you so much for this insightful discussion.

Theoretical insights

What stood out clearly for me in this discussion is Virginia's contribution to promoting cultural democracy, defined by Distinguished Professor Delores P. Aldridge (2000: 95) as the capacity to make and implement decisions and 'the capacity to define oneself as an active participant in the world rather than a passive victim'. Aldridge emphasizes the importance of recognizing the link between knowledge, culture and power, and acknowledging 'the destructive and oppressive nature of cultural domination and marginalization' (Aldridge, 2000: 101). Virginia's work in community engagement serves an important purpose in creating voice and visibility for Austin's historically marginalized Black, indigenous and Latinx communities through the powerful medium of storytelling, which is both cathartic for the communities and educational for the university and wider society. In giving voice to these communities, self-empowerment occurs through the agency that voice generates. Creating voice and visibility through the university's resources facilitates a form of restitution, an important step towards the reckoning that is so necessary to move from inequity to equity. Virginia's work through the Front Porch approach is an excellent example of how storytelling can facilitate emancipatory research through co-labouring, which acknowledges the intellectual capital that already exists in communities of colour.

References

Aldridge, D.P. (2000) 'On race and culture: Beyond Afrocentrism, Eurocentrism to cultural democracy'. *Sociological Focus*, 33 (1), 95–107.

Black British Academics (2019) 'BBA founder interviewed on Kazi Radio, Austin on Ivory Tower'. Online. https://blackbritishacademics.co.uk/2019/08/11/bba-founder-interviewed-on-kazi-radio-austin-on-ivory-tower/ (accessed 12 January 2020).

Tang, E. and Ren, C. (2014) 'Outlier: The case of Austin's declining African-American population'. Austin: Institute for Urban Policy Research and Analysis, University of Texas at Austin.

Vincent, G.J., Cumberbatch, V.A. and Blair, L.A. (eds) (2018) *As We Saw It: The story of integration at the University of Texas at Austin*. Austin: University of Texas Press.

Chapter 10

Critical reflections on transforming the Ivory Tower and beyond, part 2

Shirley Anne Tate

Looking back to the IT1 process of writing, co-editing, co-launching and supporting, I think it is necessary for me to reflect on the importance of our loving sisterhood. Love is something that we are often starved of in the academic contexts in which we find ourselves. We sometimes cannot even be respected as a fall-back position. White supremacy sees to that. Being a part of the co-production of IT1 showed me what the love of sisters in struggle looks like, feels like and can do. I cannot tell you what a relief it was for me to be in the company of Black women academics who understood what I felt, who reflected that back to me and to whom I did not have to explain or defend my thoughts and feelings in fine detail. IT1 made me feel supported in my view that something was amiss in our academic world and it wasn't about me.

It wasn't about me. Repeating that makes me see again how it is that we experience racism in a way that seeps into us unwanted and unnoticed. We become individuated. Cut off from our support structures, our sisters in struggle who would understand, sisters from whom we can ask for and receive the unconditional love we need to survive the institutions within which we make our living. We do need to make a living but at what cost to our health, wellbeing and feelings of self-worth? I have asked myself these questions repeatedly over the decades and the same answer keeps returning.

We must not leave until we are ready to do that. It is a matter of politics and communal survival. Remember what it felt like the first time you saw a Black academic or academic of colour? Do you think about the first time you were taught by one and what that felt like to you? For me, it was a liberating experience. It showed me that another academy was possible. We need new generations of Black academics and academics of colour to take up the struggle for liberation in academic life. What IT1 taught me as I looked at the audience at our book launches is, we still have work to do even if we are near the end of our careers. Love and caring for others through mentoring means that we take responsibility for how people attach to our ideas politically. They cannot be abandoned.

Aisha Richards

After decades of social justice pedagogy and activism, I found taking stock of my journey both painful and reinvigorating. As I reminisced, I realized that although I have contributed significantly to my institution in terms of cultural change and have watched many of those I have supported grow and blossom, I still sit within the skin of my Black womanhood with a constant target on my back. It has been a major challenge to fend off numerous attempts to appropriate my work, my intellectual capital and my sense of self. Irrespective of the sector, I know that other Black women across the UK will relate to knowing that no matter what you do, how others see and engage with you is different. Often the difference results in aggression towards you, whether in the form of micro-aggression, passive aggression or direct aggression, and then those who oppress us wonder why we are angry, suffer from depression and anxiety, and die early compared to our counterparts.

To reflect and share parts of my journey with Black British Academics through the Black Sister Network has built upon the sisterhood I have shared with Dr Deborah Gabriel for over a decade. In her approach to both publications Dr Gabriel has been thoughtful, motivational and supportive. Her approach has been embraced by all my fellow sisters who have contributed to the project. I had the privilege of receiving affirmation that I am not the source of my pain, nor do I have a chip on my shoulder, and this has been liberating, for which I am full of gratitude to my fellow sisters. My biggest challenge is writing about my work when I see myself as having a *doer* identity. Defining oneself as a doer means linking one's identity with the very process of behaving, independently of outcomes. Thus, having an accessible doer identity provides me with an important motivational resource that has not been explicitly recognized by existing theories (Houser-Marko and Sheldon, 2006). Writing is also a challenge when one has to consider what to share and what to withhold. My contribution to IT2 sits comfortably with creating through collaboration (Beltrán and Mehrotra, 2015) in my discussion with Dr Gabriel on one of my most significant programmes delivered through Shades of Noir, Teaching Within. I hope this discussion offers useful insights into the programme and inspires other Black British female academics to create programmes of hope for us all.

REFERENCES

Beltrán, R. and Mehrotra, G. (2015) 'Honoring our intellectual ancestors: A feminist of color treaty for creating allied collaboration'. *Affilia*, 30 (1), 106–16.

Houser-Marko, L. and Sheldon, K.M. (2006) 'Motivating behavioral persistence: The self-as-doer construct'. *Personality and Social Psychology Bulletin*, 32 (8), 1037–49.

Virginia Cumberbatch

When I think of the power of Black women, it is our world view that is intrinsically intersectional and multi-dimensional. The heightened visibility we have seen over the last few years is a result of sitting in a crescent of change. However, we will not see equity in housing, wealth, education or leadership, until our voices and our experience are included. I believe that as Black women we have grown accustomed to merely existing in decision-making spaces, fearful of stepping on toes or being the one to raise our hand to call out disparities and unfairness, rather than leveraging our unique and magical positions to be brokers of change.

Black women have always been present, proactive and powerful, yet we still struggle to position ourselves and must constantly rationalize why we should have a seat at the table. The Ivory Tower project provides a critical space to acknowledge, affirm and advance the discourse of the persistent invisibility of Black Diasporic women. It also offers a refreshing platform for us to not merely have a seat at the master's table, but to build our own. I am constantly amazed by our ability to both be consciousness-raisers and, when necessary, hell-raisers. I am inspired by this courage and conviction and I am honoured to contribute to IT2, knowing that more than ever, our experiences across the colonized world are interwoven and interdependent.

Conclusion
Deborah Gabriel

As articulated in the introduction, this edited volume is primarily aimed at Black women and women of colour, to highlight our contributions to the higher education sector, the wider society and to the causes of social justice and equity. Through critically reflective and analytical narratives that tell of our endeavours, our challenges and our achievements, we hope our stories might provide inspiration. These narratives are also a celebration and acknowledgement of the work that we do, which in many cases is pioneering and innovative. However, while the focus of these chapters is the case studies of our work, it is impossible to advance these theoretical narratives without re-living painful experiences and episodes in our academic and professional lives. These recollections bring a variety of emotions including anger, frustration, disappointment and, at times, profound sadness. However, the beauty of Black feminism is the non-linear way in which it promotes clarity, critical consciousness and agency, and facilitates self-empowerment. The edginess and brutal honesty expressed in the chapters are evidence of this paradoxical process of transformation where pain is part of the necessary transgression that precedes liberation. As the critical reflections demonstrate, this research has been transformative for us, in pushing the boundaries defiantly to reclaim our intellectual capital, which is too often appropriated:

> Academic production of feminist theory formulated in hierarchical settings often enables women, particularly White women, with high status and visibility to draw upon the work of feminist scholars who may have less or no visibility, without giving recognition to these sources. (hooks, 1994: 62)

Such appropriation of Black feminist theory can be partly attributed to the increasingly marketized, bureaucratized, capitalist environment within academia, which commodifies our intellectual capital and reproduces neo-colonial power relations:

> With the increasing institutionalization and professionalization of feminist work focused on the construction of feminist theory and the dissemination of feminist knowledge, White women have assumed positions of power that enable them to reproduce

the servant-served paradigm in a radically different context. Now Black women are placed in the position of serving White female desire to know more about race and racism, to 'master' the subject... Drawing on the work of Black women, work that they once dismissed as irrelevant, they now reproduce the servant-served paradigms in their scholarship. (hooks, 1994: 104)

The Ivory Tower project and the knowledge it produces come from a place of pain and trauma and reflect the *process* of Black feminism, which requires active participation in processes of empowerment. We therefore call upon White male and female academics not to use our work descriptively in a way that merely increases their privilege through the kudos they gain from appearing progressive when citing our work in journals that are peer-reviewed predominantly by White academics. Black feminist theory, as it has been created here, is to be practised. For those colleagues and contemporaries who consider themselves to be anti-racists, it means undertaking actions that acknowledge your White privilege and makes some form of redress. We want to engage in meaningful dialogues and collaborations with White colleagues but refuse to engage with tokenistic gestures that make no real contribution to challenging the status quo. I therefore conclude this volume with the following recommendation: instead of writing about race and gender inequality and citing (though often not citing) the work of Black feminists (when we are perfectly capable of theorizing our own experiences), think of how you can contribute towards material changes in our lives. How will you enhance our voice and visibility and acknowledge our contributions? How will you advocate for fair remuneration and career opportunities for Black women and women of colour? How will you contribute to critical and inclusive pedagogy and how will you deal with your privilege? We look forward to meaningful dialogues in the future on these important questions.

REFERENCES

hooks, b. (1994) *Teaching to Transgress: Education as the practice of freedom.* London: Routledge.

Index